The Opposite of Seduction

The Opposite of Seduction
—New Poetry in German—

Edited by
Alexander Kappe
Nicola Thomas &
Jana Maria Weiß

Shearsman Books

First published in the United Kingdom in 2025 by
Shearsman Books Ltd, P.O. Box 4239, Swindon SN3 9FN

Shearsman Books Ltd Registered Office: 30-31 St James Place,
Mangotsfield, Bristol BS16 9JB *(this address not for correspondence)*

EU AUTHORISED REPRESENTATIVE:
Lightning Source France 1 Av. Johannes Gutenberg, 78310 Maurepas, France
Email: compliance@lightningsource.fr

ISBN 978-1-84861-888-6

www.shearsman.com

Selection copyright © Alexander Kappe, Nicola Thomas and
Jana Maria Weiß, 2025; *Introduction* copyright © Nicola Thomas, 2025

Copyright in the poems printed in this volume rests with their authors and are copyright © 2025, except where otherwise cited in the acknowledgements on pages 198-201, which constitute an extension of this copyright page.

The rights of the authors of the introduction and of the poems in this book to be identified as the authors thereof have been asserted by them in accordance with the Copyrights, Designs and Patents Act of 1988. All rights reserved.

Cover image: Andrea Büttner, *Potatoes*, 2019. Gouache on cardboard. 69.2 x 50 x 0.2 cm © Andrea Büttner. Image by courtesy of the artist and Hollybush Gardens, London.

This book has been selected to receive financial assistance from English PEN's PEN Translates programme, supported by Arts Council England. English PEN exists to promote literature and our understanding of it, to uphold writers' freedoms around the world, to campaign against the persecution and imprisonment of writers for stating their views, and to promote the friendly co-operation of writers and the free exchange of ideas. www.englishpen.org).

The work of the translators was supported by a grant of the German Translators' Fund as part of the programme NEUSTART KULTUR by the Federal Government Commissioners for Culture and Media.

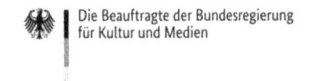

CONTENTS

Introduction / Nicola Thomas   11

HEART

the opposite of seduction / Monika Rinck   17
   (trans. Nicholas Grindell)
from Thicket with Speeches and Eyes / Steffen Popp   18
   (trans. Bradley Schmidt)
from the clearance of these parks / Daniel Falb   19
   (trans. Robert Gillett)
Size, Procrastination / Ann Cotten *(trans. Ann Cotten)*   20
ratinger hof, documentary report 1 / Thomas Kling
   (trans. Andrew Duncan)   22
ratinger hof, documentary report 2 / Thomas Kling
   (trans. Andrew Duncan)   23
final signals / Nadja Küchenmeister *(trans. Aimee Chor)*   24
putto or person / Georg Leß *(trans. Alexander Kappe)*   25
Extension, Possession / Ann Cotten *(trans. Ann Cotten)*   26
Elegy for K. / Steffen Popp *(trans. Donna Stonecipher)*   27
Life Repeats Itself / Tom Schulz *(trans. Gerald Fiebig)*   28

BODY

displacement of the mouth / Uljana Wolf *(trans. Grace Nissan)*   31
my training objectives / Monika Rinck *(trans. Nicholas Grindell)*   32
In My Estimation / Elke Erb *(trans. Shane Anderson)*   33
skin / Sabine Scho *(trans. Catherine Hales)*   34
a battlefield of legs / Carolin Callies *(trans. Paul-Henri Campbell)*   35
from the clearance of these parks / Daniel Falb   36
   (trans. Robert Gillett)
Homology, Myself / Ann Cotten *(trans. Ann Cotten)*   37
from the clearance of these parks / Daniel Falb   38
   (trans. Robert Gillett)
pray how does getting ready work? / Monika Rinck   39
   (trans. Nicholas Grindell)
for daphne: lamented / Anja Utler *(trans. Kurt Beals)*   40
seven / Kerstin Preiwuss *(trans. Bradley Schmidt)*   43
Dealings With Gaps / Peter Waterhouse *(trans. Iain Galbraith)*   44

SOUL

Heidelberg, Hotel / Elke Erb (trans. Shane Anderson)	47
Sitting in the Garden without Equivalent / Peter Waterhouse (trans. Iain Galbraith)	48
Window to the World Night / Steffen Popp (trans. Bradley Schmidt)	49
Kingdom of the Swallowed Shell / Yevgeniy Breyger (trans. Alexander Kappe)	50
Kingdom of Rain / Yevgeniy Breyger (trans. Alexander Kappe)	51
Kingdom of the Distant Path / Yevgeniy Breyger (trans. Alexander Kappe)	52
on two trees / Birgit Kreipe (trans. Shane Anderson)	53
from Seven Dignitites. Notre Dame de Paris et des Fleurs April 15, 2019 ff., o / Alexandru Bulucz (trans. Jake Schneider)	54
In a state of imponderability / Jayne-Ann Igel (trans. Karen Leeder)	55
Self-Portrait Next to a Renaissance Window / Steffen Popp (trans. Bradley Schmidt)	56
Self-Portrait with Aspic / Hendrik Jackson (trans. Alexander Kappe)	57
from 'A Letter, after 35 Years' / Dinçer Güçyeter (trans. Caroline Wilcox Reul)	58
SAGA / Daniela Seel (trans. Shane Anderson)	59

BEAST

dust bunnies vs. wool mice / Uljana Wolf (trans. Sophie Seita)	65
On the Day of the Narrow Thought / Peter Waterhouse (trans. Iain Galbraith)	66
Boramets – The Vegetable Lamb / Sebastian Unger (trans. Ann Cotten)	67
tweeting is a tiny beast / Carolin Callies (trans. Paul-Henri Campbell)	68
what about the animals? / Monika Rinck (trans. Nicholas Grindell)	69
The Child's Report / Christoph Meckel (trans. Bradley Schmidt)	70
In the House Opposite / Jan Kuhlbrodt (trans. Alexander Kappe)	71
falconry / Thomas Kling (trans. Andrew Duncan)	73
a tropical orchid, wild, in his beake / Friederike Mayröcker (trans. Nicola Thomas)	74

orpheus charms beasts of lesser quality / MONIKA RINCK   75
(trans. Nicholas Grindell)
The Untied Tamer / SEBASTIAN UNGER *(trans. Ann Cotten)*   76
Ling / VERENA STAUFFER *(trans. Bradley Schmidt)*   77
supercortemaggiore! / MONIKA RINCK *(trans. Nicholas Grindell)*   78
stranded sperm whale / SABINE SCHO *(trans. Ann Cotten)*   79

SEASON

deep blue may, seething / FRIEDERIKE MAYRÖCKER   83
(trans. Nicola Thomas)
from Going to the Woods, Stealing Timber for a Bed /   84
MARTINA HEFTER *(trans. Karen Leeder)*
from Going to the Woods, Stealing Timber for a Bed /   85
MARTINA HEFTER *(trans. Karen Leeder)*
Fir Trees, the Borderland / STEFFEN POPP *(trans. Bradley Schmidt)*   86
Green border / JAYNE-ANN IGEL *(trans. Karen Leeder)*   87
december is a rhino / BIRGIT KREIPE *(trans. Joel Scott & Lotta Thießen)*   88
Summering / OSWALD EGGER *(trans. Iain Galbraith)*   89
freeze frame / HENDRIK JACKSON *(trans. Catherine Hales)*   91
Conversations with Tree Bark II / ALEXANDRU BULUCZ   92
(trans. Jake Schneider)
The Gabion/Ecogravilla / ANN COTTEN *(trans. Ann Cotten)*   94
from études / FRIEDERIKE MAYRÖCKER *(trans. Donna Stonecipher)*   97
the last day down south / MONIKA RINCK   98
(trans. Nicholas Grindell)
it begins where it ends / NADJA KÜCHENMEISTER   99
(trans. Aimee Chor)

MAP

Doubts About Trams / PETER WATERHOUSE *(trans. Iain Galbraith)*   103
from CEK / DANIEL FALB *(trans. Robert Gillett)*   104
from My Prince, I am the Ghetto / DINÇER GÜÇYETER   105
(trans. Caroline Wilcox Reul)
To the Last Meal by Memory Carriage I / ALEXANDRU BULUCZ   106
(trans. Jake Schneider)
Crișcior Straw Road / ALEXANDRU BULUCZ *(trans. Jake Schneider)*   107
ICE / Ann Cotten *(trans. Ann Cotten)*   108
After the Rifle Fire II / STEFFEN POPP *(trans. Bradley Schmidt)*   109
protection from stalking – as i imagine it / HENDRIK JACKSON   110
(trans. Alexander Kappe)

Ashen Gold Ash / Christoph Meckel *(trans. Bradley Schmidt)* 111
Auratic Agrology / Steffen Popp *(trans. Christian Hawkey)* 112
The blue blood of the rivers' courses / Jayne-Ann Igel 114
   (trans. Karen Leeder)
From Peace without War / Yevgeniy Breyger 115
   (trans. Alexander Kappe)
Circle Train / Tom Schulz *(trans. Gerald Fiebig)* 116

MACHINE

from 'Songs of the Radio Tower' / Ulrike Almut Sandig 119
   (trans. Karen Leeder)
from the clearance of these parks / Daniel Falb 121
   (trans. Brian Currid)
Sonar's Supper of Wrath / Sonja vom Brocke 122
   (trans. Catherine Hales)
Little Windmill / Christoph Meckel *(trans. Bradley Schmidt)* 123
fifth vertebra / we beleaguered / Georg Leß *(trans. Chris Fenwick)* 124
from The Origin of Values / Sabine Scho *(trans. Bradley Schmidt)* 125
Theory of Signs (B. F. Electrics) / Sebastian Unger 127
   (trans. Alexander Kappe)
be brave, moon / Dagmara Kraus *(trans. Joshua Daniel Edwin)* 128
from CEK / Daniel Falb *(trans. Christian Hawkey)* 129
Aircraft Cleared for Take-Off / Sabine Scho *(trans. Karen Leeder)* 130

LORE

Lore / Sonja vom Brocke *(trans. Catherine Hales)* 133
witch k / Birgit Kreipe *(trans. Catherine Hales)* 134
Footnotes from the Margins of Antiquity / Steffen Popp 136
   (trans. Bradley Schmidt)
serner, carlsbad / Thomas Kling *(trans. Andrew Duncan)* 137
Ghosts / Thomas Kling *(trans. Andrew Duncan)* 138
training session with the white man / Birgit Kreipe 139
   (trans. Catherine Hales)
the forty-five bloodjesus legends / Ulf Stolterfoht 141
   (trans. Catherine Hales)

HOME

stationary / Uljana Wolf *(trans. Sophie Seita)* 151
The Working Class Queues up at Lidl in the Evening / 152
   Tom Schulz *(trans. Gerald Fiebig)*

hiding / ULRIKE DRAESNER *(trans. Iain Galbraith)*	154
The Mini Monks / DINÇER GÜÇYETER *(trans. Caroline Wilcox Reul)*	155
at the base / NADJA KÜCHENMEISTER *(trans. Aimee Chor)*	156
from fugitive moons / YEVGENIY BREYGER *(trans. Alexander Kappe)*	157
a white shoelace- / CHRISTIAN FILIPS *(trans. Jayashree Hari Joshi)*	158
In Praise of a Room / PETER WATERHOUSE *(trans. Iain Galbraith)*	159
Ecstasy for Outsiders / SEBASTIAN UNGER *(trans. Alexander Kappe)*	161
The Green Cardigan / DINÇER GÜÇYETER *(trans. Caroline Wilcox Reul)*	162
from fugitive moons / YEVGENIY BREYGER *(trans. Alexander Kappe)*	164
this is my claim / BIRGIT KREIPE *(trans. Catherine Hales)*	166
my gutless gob, muted by misery / MONIKA RINCK *(trans. Nicholas Grindell)*	167

POEM

little star-nosed mole speech / ULJANA WOLF *(trans. Sophie Seita)*	171
Deliberation / ELKE ERB *(trans. Amy Visram & Jana Maria Weiß)*	172
Begging Sentence for Clarity / CHRISTIAN FILIPS *(trans. Shane Anderson)*	173
who is taking notes / GEORG LESS *(trans. Alexander Kappe)*	174
Shelf 1 / JAN KUHLBRODT *(trans. Alexander Kappe)*	175
from HOW TO DO TE T(H)**INK**ERING / ULRIKE DRAESNER *(trans. Iain Galbraith)*	178
Measured Gaze / ANN COTTEN *(trans. Ann Cotten)*	182
Traversability / ELKE ERB *(trans. Amy Visram & Jana Maria Weiß)*	184
what is poetry? / ULRIKE DRAESNER *(trans. Iain Galbraith)*	185
from gloomerang / DAGMARA KRAUS *(trans. Joshua Daniel Edwin)*	187
to the dogs of kreisau / ULJANA WOLF *(trans. Brian Currid)*	189
postscript to the kreisau dogs / ULJANA WOLF *(trans. Brian Currid)*	190
Suspicion of a Poem / ELKE ERB *(trans. Shane Anderson)*	191
About the authors and translators	192
Acknowledgements	198
Index of Poets	202
Index of Translators	203

INTRODUCTION

Nicola Thomas

English-language readers have relatively few opportunities to encounter contemporary German-language poetry; the simple purpose of this anthology is to offer one such opportunity, in the form of a selection of recent poems translated from the German for an English-language audience. It has been noted that the last twenty or so years have been a moment of great vitality for the German-language lyric, much of the excitement of which has passed English-speaking countries by, for want of translations, and particularly for want of a selection of translated works gathered in one place. It is our hope that the poems presented here speak largely for themselves: that they offer range and variety, something for (almost) everyone, that they make visible some lines of connection in terms of form, style and theme—and, above all, that they show English-speaking readers a glimpse of the vibrancy of the German-language lyric in the first part of the twenty-first century.

The selection here was in one sense guided by the desire to present a genealogy of German poetry starting with three senior figures: Elke Erb, Thomas Kling and Friederike Mayröcker. These three poets—two German (one East, one West) and one Austrian, and in themselves also quite different—have an enduring influence on German-language poetry. A kind of stripped back collage-form; an interest in language itself, and in the fact of the poem; a poetics which is at once both sparse and generous, which blends material and abstract, and which is ultimately often playful in effect: these are some of the hallmarks of the strands of contemporary German poetry represented here, and which reveal the multiple and overlapping legacies of these three late twentieth-century giants, samples of whose work are also included.

There are, as always with such projects, many omissions and oversights, and the final selection here is as idiosyncratic and personal as the taste of the editors. What emerges, we hope, is a sense not only of the thrilling transformation of German poetry mentioned above, but also some idea of where the recent boom came from and how it has unfolded across several decades. We have stopped short of the absolute latest generation of writers for pragmatic reasons: no doubt a future anthology will record this very active scene which continues to flourish.

There are marked similarities between the current vibrancy of certain subsections of English-language poetry and the corresponding German-language scenes. A major factor in the emergence of new poetries in both contexts is the rise of small-press and DIY publishers, relying on laptops and keeping costs low, oriented towards friendship circles and coteries. That artists and writers of all kinds could live affordably in German cities—particularly Berlin—for at least the first decade of the twenty-first century also contributed to the rise of indie publishers such as kookbooks, gutleut, roughbooks, Poetenladen, Edition Korrespondenzen, ELIF or Verlagshaus Berlin who first published many of the poets we include here (and for whose cooperation in the current project we are extremely grateful). More recently, different circumstances have led to the flourishing of poetry scenes in places such as Munich, Vienna, Frankfurt and Leipzig.

Thematically, too, readers of contemporary English-language poetry will spot overlaps which speak to what are, increasingly, concerns that resonate around the globe: the relationship of humans to the places, to the world, in which we live; the political and technological context of bodies and bodily encounter (across the spectrum of friendship, love, and sex); the unfolding of history and its intersection with personal identity, including in the context of migration; and the status and reliability of language and of poetry itself. At the same time, what makes these poems rewarding to the Anglophone reader is seeing familiar themes refracted through a new set of perspectives, in the context of a different lyric tradition. The poems here which deal with nature and environment illustrate this perfectly, speaking (quite literally) a different language from that of Hughes or Heaney—and thus seeing the world in a different way.

Common to Anglophone and German-language poetry since at least 2000, and probably earlier, is a crisis of relevance brought about the marginal role poetry plays in today's literary marketplace. After modernism, what is poetry for? Contrasting answers to this question came from those following in the footsteps of seventies and eighties avant-gardes, and by those who favoured a more direct, politically engaged poetry. Art for art's sake, or committed writing? German-language writers, drawing perhaps on their strong Romantic heritage, have often attempted to find a middle way. Mixing registers is central to some of the poems presented here; profound questions are treated humorously, everyday problems with deadly seriousness. Pathos and bathos go hand in hand. The boundary between prose and poetry is also blurred, and several of these writers turn to narrative techniques. The tradition of nature poetry is put to the test; sometimes it is used as a foil for the speaker's inner life, but at other times nature itself is made to speak instead being spoken of. Finally, the relationship of truth and fiction is called into question. Can a poem be 'lyrical research'? Is poetry, as Monika Rinck wrote in an essay, actually 'non-fiction'?

There are poems here which may test the boundaries of Anglophone tastes. In particular, readers may be interested in reflecting on the long-standing tension in German poetry between the poetry of ideas, *Gedankenlyrik*, and *Erlebnislyrik*, the poetry of experience. Since British and North American readers' tastes tend to run towards the concrete and experiential, some of the more conceptual work here may puzzle or even irritate. Nonetheless, as editors, we were keen to present a broad cross-section—again, with an eye to what was otherwise little available in English, which includes many fine poems in the tradition of *Gedankenlyrik*.

It is, perhaps, these poems of ideas which most test the skills of the translator. We are particularly proud that our anthology gives space to a very wide range of translators, nearly as many as there are authors, from the most accomplished and well-known mediators of German-language poetry into English, such as Karen Leeder and Iain Galbraith, to those who seldom translate or are at the start of their translating career. Many and varied approaches to translation are on display, from those which are relatively free interpretations, prioritising sound and mood; to those which aim for maximum precision in the rendering of sense or imagery. Throughout, UK and US spellings and styles are used according to the translator's preference. All translations are new poems, rather than transparent windows to the 'original' text, and we encourage you to read these poems as such. For this reason, and in order to squeeze in as many poems as possible, we have also opted not to include parallel texts in German.

Finally, some notes on the selection of poets and poems. The large majority are German—some born in the East, some in the West, and many born in and identifying with the modern, unified nation state. Some are migrants to Germany who did not grow up speaking German; some are German with parents or grandparents from elsewhere. A few (notably Mayröcker, one of the volume's key points of orientation) are Austrian. We present the poets collectively in this way, rather than insisting on differences of national or other affiliation, in order to show commonalities and invite comparison of how different poets draw on and replenish the shared linguistic resources of the German language.

The grouping of the poems into sections with thematic titles is relatively unusual for an English-language anthology, where poems tend to be grouped by poet or chronologically. Thematic groupings such as those we use here, are, however, common in German-language anthologies, and seemed a habit worth adopting, a way of inviting comparison, exploration and curiosity.

This project was supported by grants given by English PEN and the Deutscher Übersetzerfonds (German Translators' Fund), with the support of the Neustart Kultur programme of the Bundesbeauftragte für Kultur und Medien (BKM) (Federal Commission for Culture and Media). Additional funding to support the preparation of the publication was provided by Lancaster University. We are grateful to Karen Leeder for her advice and guidance, and to Rey Conquer for editorial support. We would also like to thank Tony Frazer of Shearsman Books for agreeing to take this project on, and doing so much to ensure it came to fruition. Finally, we are grateful to Andrea Büttner for permission to use her work on the cover, and to Monika Rinck for allowing us to borrow her playful, suggestive title, *The Opposite of Seduction*, as the title of our volume.

HEART

MONIKA RINCK
the opposite of seduction

this drying out, is it some belated protest against the march of time?
and this imperceptible growth in spite of bad treatment: for years
now i've been tipping the rancid remains from the cups – more
coffee anyone? – into the pots, or not watering them at all
for weeks on end, loose woody stalks in some excuse for soil.
the way they keep growing, or at least pretend to: they parody life.
and into my back they soundlessly heft their rickety swords,
put out of joint in transit from one office to another. they slouch
in corners, engaged in gloom and photosynthesis. what moments
ago was cooling the chip is now being used by our eight-hour lungs.
what sort of plant is that? heidrun brought it. they've bred dogs
without hair, yes they have, but plants without leaves? i stand
before this plant and into the computers' hum i say: "forevermore
my dwelling place shall be". and think of outside, a wind, gentle,
the leaves, the leaves, moving as one and among their own kind,
and this single ugly plant here as a redeemer figure, so that all of us,
all of us rise again into an age now obsolete, where we don't sow,
don't reap, just bide our time in the opposite of seduction. they all say:
i'll bring some peat tomorrow. the morrow comes. no one brings peat.

Nicholas Grindell

STEFFEN POPP
from *Thicket with Speeches and Eyes*

Stepping out of the concrete, entirely rabbit fur.
Touching the rough glove, turning it inside out.
Moving something like pebbles slowly in your mouth.

The head, the buried cloud form.
The heart, the doubled, enormous sack form.

Concrete was thought, a school
massive. A bell's inside enveloped in sleep. Sleep
however, was another.

With milky white feet, rolled back like eyes
with conjunctivitis, under down.

We lay, I believe, in both
and sometimes in both at once.

Did I ever meet you, besides in sleep, hours before the dew fell
which we, crazy for depth, kissed from stones?
The heart was these stones, you say.
Yet, and against them: I don't think so.

Bradley Schmidt

DANIEL FALB
from *the clearance of these parks*

to casualty of course i was not admitted.
      repeating myself so often was a bad move.
but as far as the archers the anamneses
      soughed as script from hamlet to
hamlet. a geographical scenario,
      in this quarter wilhelm conrad röntgen
thought up the sunbed, the stage fright
      before the performance. orange was still going strong,
although, speaking parts there were none here
      in the open air, just waiting for the call.

Robert Gillett

THOMAS KLING
ratinger hof, documentary report 1

for juliette

hands that crave for rich,
for - shift of continents - zip
fasteners: pill hands,
acid   "I AM AVAILABLE NIGHTS"
in the crush my hand grows
around the glass, later around her
shoulder; her 19 year old on-off
switch grows towards me; "I AM NOT
AVAILABLE NIGHTS" teeth snip
my optic nerve, it all splashes up
against my leather armour, counter optic
nerve, against her naked shoulder,
against the teeth of the zips
"SEA": the insect crush;
out of the throats of wasps splashes slogan
on slogan, splashes the
sting, stab "SLEEP" the
sharpened:
         LET THE PRINT STAMPER STAMP/
RIGHT AWAY THE CHINESE HOROSCOPE/SEND
ME YOUR HOPI TELEGRAM/I'LL GIVE YOU
THE WORD GAROTTE SO YOU CAN TRY
IT OUT ON ME/"QUOTE MARKS"/I
CANT LIVE WITHOUT THE WORD PRRSHNG
LEDDA PRISTAMPER TMP I feel her
deautifully black antennae I want to get
rid of my beautifully yellow one I give her the
slogan

Andrew Duncan

THOMAS KLING
ratinger hof, documentary report 2

*If your mother only knew that
Her heart would burst in her body...*

UNDER THE -KICKERTOBITS the dancing your shoes to death;
carefully waxed calves in front of crates
of bock-beer bottles; the the kicking to bits
bulletin from dragée pupils, -skins,
decibel throbs; crashed bulletin
through milky glass, that's it, through partition
panes ; jerking iris, shaved pubis,
decibel throbs, stamping light to bits the the
kicking apart in her "boots must die"
boots;
        waltz is now the pogo! vulcanite
against PVC! get with it! you bags with
the the slipped out catheters with the in
grown unpainted with the the
nails on toes on sharp feet on bedridden
in there in the old people's nursing home
                            (I see informing
through partition panes – nothing more
from dragée pupils from tablet hand from
congested skin from crumbling gums behind
blue lips; but one more thing their verd
verdun their verdun look end of
bulletin) decibel throbs, plucked eyebrows.
under the heel of light the the dancing to bits
IN THE THIRD STAGE EVEN ONANISM NO
LONGER WORKS THE PATIENT HAS NO N
EED FOR GENITAL ACTIVITY A SI
GHT A SMELL A TOUCH OR LIC
KING OR KISSING THE SHOE SUFFICE

Andrew Duncan

NADJA KÜCHENMEISTER
final signals

the hall is dark and long, as a hall
not quite convincing, one finds
the shoes to be calming, polite

in a row, worn down, the wardrobe grabs
at one's throat, a hand that threatens collapse
under the weight of coats and scarves, plastic

bags, grocery store, year after year, when
will it break? the door to the kitchen ajar
the fridge could stand to be defrosted

the radio on the windowsill, raining
you start your life so small, the broken
antenna keeps searching for signals

that no one can remember
behind the door is in front of the shelves, one walks
down the hall, and what then?

Aimee Chor

GEORG LESS
putto or person

mouldable like marzipan, we mould each other into other
people's children, out of convenience, but I invest my lifetime and tear
with a thirst for elevation and tick tweezers
in my slender shadow, it's swarming short and dandy
war elephants, they would come in more handy

one tears longer, until tension breaks, shifts to snaking
reward follows on the ground, bunch of keys found, two-room flat, moved

I miss, I am
already forgetting them

putto or person

Alexander Kappe

ANN COTTEN
Extension, Possession

Your name has widened, and yet just a while ago:
Instants ago, I mean, you were a newfound sound to me.
Now I can hardly read a phrase without you, go
ahead and come, I miss the rest, no need

to say a thing: the quiet holds your teeth;
the rhyme evaporates, the rhythm flounders, there you stand,
your ankles garnished with a sonnet wreath.
The concept of you curtsies and I come around

and my approach conceals the way you disappear
as I sing lonely verses to your back,
the prettiest part of you, or am I just pretending
to be able to ignore you the way you ignore me?
'cause when you talk, it's like into a sack.
I'd carry it away, but where? You're like a machine, venting

the heat you use to cool the part that works.
I look for how you act in all my tricks,
but must be different. I try talking on and on, that sucks:
my pitcher keeps pouring itself upon your ball-like rocks.

You quietly start testing individual words.
I notice right away, but still finish my sentence.
You ask if you can say something and I say, sure.
Our lips meet; one of us two may be doing penance.

You bend the world I live in like a raving stick;
I love you and you're worried about ticks.
My cheek recalls your chin; I know it must itch.
I know, in theory, how to pronounce your name.
I see you stand before me with no sign of shame,
showing me your back side exactly how it is.

Ann Cotten

STEFFEN POPP
Elegy for K.

Tired is my eye, tired tired
like Alps. An enchanted distance
of years is my face,
fields, in which I slept –

yellow Chinese lanterns, a puzzling children's party
everything is outside me, a reservoir
in which flooded towns glow at night.

The earth gives colors
the skin gives unity
in the plantations the fruit-trees are valiantly armed
against the universe –

all around, the meadows
                rub against my feet
the river by my side
is pulled, imperceptibly,
by a far sea.

Donna Stonecipher

TOM SCHULZ
Life Repeats Itself

Having to do the shopping eventually
one sits and sees how the sky
looks today:
a blue wonder, a yellow misery?

Nothing repeats itself.

However: trees in public parks.
A long-time acquaintance of grass.
Other people's children will never be
as beautiful.

Does the kiss repeat, the fingers
in the hair, the hand over the eyes?

Nothing repeats itself.

In the morning, the car tyres crunch
and a boozehound
hops from the gap.

That I love you is a paraphrase
of the ships that lie in the harbour.

Gerald Fiebig

BODY

SABINE SCHO
skin

acid protection and
pressure sensitivity,
just show me your
leg, a heart-shaped
bruise, my business,
what's it got to do with
you, exercises in identi-
fying matters of involve-
ment, but caring went
missing a long time ago,
covering the whole area
of an overarm, a sparkling
a hissing cloaking the
laughter, that has to
soak in first, the epi-
critical places, wait
i'll hold the ice pack

Catherine Hales

CAROLIN CALLIES
a battlefield of legs

whom had i summoned before you, when the berserkers died?
what stood fast: nothing more than a leg covered by bruises
& we carried it out & put it in
& the leg was swollen, tarred, & feathered
including the leaflet for more cadavers on foot.

for goodness sake, is there anyone
who could hire that horde?
more dust could settle on them
& we'd cross our swords again & we'd blacken the tips
& we'd have them hunt for wild boars & we'd reduce everything to rubble.

who should i imagine now, when i envision you without legs?
we're constantly clearing our throats. was it in the end just a leg full of
        harpoons
—that's how pointed its angles are. that's why it keeps together that well
& one leg is standing with me wrenched just in case.
but remains is a short word for you laying there.

Paul-Henri Campbell

DANIEL FALB
from *the clearance of these parks*

the container station was kept at body temperature,
not necessarily a sign of life.
      the money laundrette appeared here as a moult,
you stood in the nude among suds.
      we brought in the terrarium without paying duty,
and whatever sloughed its skin in there belonged henceforth to us both.
      the money laundrette appeared here as a moult,
but these things get busted.
      we had our hands full with projected expenditure.

someone was walking around out there with my kidney,
                                      and it wasn't you.
your canary bird looked so peculiar today,
      and your upper thighs were in full bloom,
but i in passing failed to notice this.

Robert Gillett

MONIKA RINCK
pray how does getting ready work?

pray how does getting ready work? how do fake tans
and hair-washing work? these are age-old questions,
surely, stretching way back down the generations,
like standing on a landing stage and eating canapés
on someone's engagement day, and a band plays,
and over and over bottles are emptied and glasses filled.
the wind changes, flutters, lays bare the triceps,
frills shimmy, flounces, hands on upper arms, verily
between champagne and flesh-tone the difference
is a sliding scale. or might it not be better (even now?)
to grapple with bodies, to rip at the glad rags
and lie in back rooms as dawn breaks outside and
truth dawns within. and then have to write something
far younger than my years that makes the otters
laugh and hold hands, ring-a-ring-o'-roses, no, no, no,
that lingerie's not mine, it must be someone else's.

Nicholas Grindell

ANJA UTLER
for daphne: lamented

> *Transformed into a laurel, Daphne,*
> *whose own name denotes the laurel,*
> *yields herself to the lover turned poet.*
>
> Karlheinz Stierle

> *The spurge laurel, like other species of*
> *Daphne, is highly poisonous. [..] The*
> *leaves resemble those of a laurel tree,*
> *hence the genus name Daphne.*
>
> www.heilpflanzensuchmaschine.de

myself: as if dethorned! by him as: if it had all
turned now am: scented, am stalked – fully: quarry my
sweat – rush: through branches, through brushwood from him
they: light into grab hook whipping – swifter –
my flanks eyes – no – (..) know: i must go through must
make it – at once – to the river, river –

–

beg him: take me quick, father, i: plunge in your
rapids and you then: release me – pure – as foam
as air, air –
and fleeing i ripple your face in thanks –

–

and, already: you spray: lap my ankles – refreshing –
will free me, let go – now, at once –

–

may not though – no –
what: are you taking –

to you, ran – straight – onto your: sodden
ground, fixed: with a single jerk, lurch, no,
limbs ripping still rear up and stop –
i must: warp myself, withered, worked: into the wood
stiffen – what are you taking from me: me

–

see, as last sight: it adorns you, my
unseeing image will, must always, glitter with you, rippled,
dimmer, now skimming: your thanks now – it swims –
in the eyes of the hunter as well

–

how dry: my arm makes – made! the flanks, often, now they
well up, out
they: salivate, gnaw – at me – mounting –
make room then: entwines himself in me: and his hot flesh –

damp! so unceasing – you rise up in me, raise me:
that i may stand, bloom and bear may: not even shed
leaves, just my: fruits fall away – unawares: so i bring them they –
rot, nourish: your ground

–

now allowed just to wither, to parch just: to thirst
hear: i rustle out drier now after the birds –

singe! please, scorch the shadow from him: from this red brow,
so that he: may burn out – this pulse: from my tips,
so that i may: release myself – pure – as a scent as uncrackling
air may submerge may submerse – myself leafing deleafing –
into: the low, spurging shoots drive them: from me
berried, spraying, stretch out – hissing: eat of it, eat –

Kurt Beals

KERSTIN PREIWUSS
seven

it's shedding today
the people say
a scraping
the people say
pure with pain
you'll revel in

growing in antlers out of
linen first then vellum then velvet
if need be

disappearing under hand
huddling under the nails
the head and the body of woman

given to me
to live on

Bradley Schmidt

PETER WATERHOUSE
Dealings with Gaps

Why did we occupy the gaps? The two ends
are unknown. The unscrambled mid-point calls:
me. Thus begin our happy dealings with gaps. Will there
be failure? O, we have already failed. Waking
up in the morning we are used to saying to ourselves: Hello
failed middling me. Today
is the next great Project Failure. Welcome.
With silver eyes (might as well shut that silver eye
already), with lips opened long before each spoken word
(they too could be clapped down early on), with fingers, ears, navel
etc. (all on the cusp of happiness – even the navel
lives in ecstatic readiness – so one should rightly say: O you navel): May I
be urged (by whom?) into the least known moment of the day, and may this
be called the day of the unknown navel: Good morning. Are all gaps
unchanged? Yes, all gaps are unchanged and in their examples lie.
You often hear the cry: Please clap out the gaps in good time, navel
etc.: Please find the best form of ecstasy. One
might almost wish to become a navel: Bounded form at
the centre. So the question is: Are we a navel?
No. Can we at least have dealings
with the navel? No, the navel is stubborn.
We have dealings with gaps. Are such dealings
pleasurable?
Yes.
No.

Iain Galbraith

SOUL

PETER WATERHOUSE
Sitting in the Garden without Equivalent

Today you said: simplify yourself. Put
differently: make a simplification and take a stand
or seat (to be referred to then as: self, sitting
in simplification. Or: your simple state
is so endearing.) The contraction could be:
world, table, armchair. Why? And:
why are we asking? Taking a seat in the armchair
is the endearing reduction (so-called reduction
without equivalent). Everything happens without
equivalent. And who sits at the centre
of such equivalentlessness? We do. We
have simplified ourselves. Sitting
thought goes: I'm sitting. I'm sitting
at the end of the row. The row goes:
world, table, armchair, me. The reason for this aspect is:
make a simplification. Seat yourself at the point
without equivalent. (The simile goes: we are not
world, table, armchair. We add ourselves to them.) The sitter calls
cheekily: Mr Reaper, I am not a flower. Answer: stand up
from the armchair, it's different; from the table
it's different; from the world, it's a stranger. At night:
you simplified overnight guest. During the day:
you simplified daytime guest. Come here
you armchair; bring yourself with you.

Iain Galbraith

STEFFEN POPP
Window to the World Night

A tram is sleeping in front of the building – yellow
with its frame folded down, curled into the sidelights

in the bow of the railcar two conductors are dreaming
headless, under the brims of their cardboard caps' visors

one moves
climbs out, a faint glowing dot, and breathes
smoke, with his back to the driver's cab

at length he looks
       up, through the orange lighting –

blind
as Homer, in black shoes
with steel toes
under the gable of Uranus.

Bradley Schmidt

YEVGENIY BREYGER
Kingdom of the Swallowed Shell

At night, as the village arms itself, rain sweeps
over branches and reveals its motive – transformation
of trees into script. Her sorrowful shirt,
the scaled shirt over her skin keeps her awake,

when she sleeps. There's still light in the valley,
soon she sits down at the table. Soon she takes the knife,
soon she carves a sign into it that helps her
to forget. By the river, stones lie in the reeds.

At night, as she becomes pregnant, she dreams
herself swapped with the child. She carries it
in front of her like a castle when it cries.
As a dress, when it's hungry, as a shell, when she's alone.

The child opens her eyes, sees itself born,
she puts a shell in it. How do I distinguish
a ward from a fist? A mist
from a mouth that is about to swallow

mist? The flat surface
of the body from a treeless steppe,
where an unborn child lies motionless?
Threads, alive, spin a web through her

heart. There's still a light in the belly,
soon a hand scoops a little water into the bowl,
makes sense of a sign, soon a knocking is heard,
opens the doors in the village – Was that me?

Alexander Kappe

YEVGENIY BREYGER
Kingdom of Rain

At night, as the village arms itself, she learns
of her destiny to shoot at the big rocks.
At the river's edge they wait like eyes. Determined
and quiet, stone creeps over stone – Away from her?

Another wrong course, coarser than sand,
powder that does not obey her. This dry vein,
can I grasp it? Fields – fields. Forests – beasts.
A memory blurs in thought. She runs

into the wind. Through the inner world, with haste
to the rock, she hears gunshots. History shoots at history,
dogs shoot themselves, village shoots town, animals
shoot plants at minerals. Muskets slide

through hands. Essences shoot at a soft
mixture of rubber and earth – flocks of birds
exist as such projectiles, she thinks,
and disappear between skies, between

the ground, in a breast. When you love so strongly,
neither arrival nor disappearance is possible.
Go out, even the rock has learned to forgive.
Go over to the people, their bodies

keep themselves alive by budding
when it gets warm. Yearlong spring,
where shall I go? Giving in may be your gain.
Forget what you do, follow a song.

Alexander Kappe

YEVGENIY BREYGER
Kingdom of the Distant Path

You knew her. She was quiet, swallowed mountains
with her gaze. The way water lilies brush past you in the dark,
turn into portals to fears, she touched you.
Like a point, a spoken word, she belongs to you.

Knowledge is useless, direction formless. Distance, duration
determine the form. The age of the earth is small. She said,
counting begins with the first song of a toad.
Movement owes its name to the path. Even before God,

a cut announces the births, you learnt.
You hold your head under water. In your face
a fish reads the refraction of light and swims away.
In the fish is a room you never leave. A door

to the realm that opens like leaves to spring.
It is cold. She circles your head as a satellite.
Circling back to the beginning, into the undergrowth,
to the den made of greetings. Until she leaves.

To wander through the valley, to roam the air,
following this scent on the back of the birds that
beguile you so. She goes out with closed lungs, open
mouth in search of wood for a nest. Since she flies,

she is heavy. That strange moment when you wake up
in a dream as a line and the dream obeys you, when
an inscription fits into the image of her open hand, that
leads to the question – Where were you when you were born?

Alexander Kappe

BIRGIT KREIPE
on two trees

what if we only turn into earth? mobile
foam or moss? or two sponges
their dead, spores under their shells?
why was i so complicated? do we just become a puff of air?
fumbling, flowing schemes, between trees
shaking down the nuts in autumn?
do we catch each other again? listen: the masterful bird—
do we just cover ourselves with night?
can a temple be dismantled into boards and light?

Shane Anderson

STEFFEN POPP
Self-Portrait Next to a Renaissance Window

The world, if not the cosmos, beheld me, its forgetting
the master builder's skull shimmered in the sunrise
by that incubator of light, a Renaissance window, I
stood, awake, behind the opaque white of my eyes

over the city, my fever reached through the congealed
gold of its towers as if through a wall of ancient rain

I vaguely followed flocks of stars, their wear and tear, felt
the moon, a hand stirring the depths, pale and
precise, while the sun rose, devastating, on the horizon

perhaps I was merely sad in time and much in space
almost nothing left of the child who struggled like marine animals
unaccompanied through earth and air and made their way late to the sea

the dead master builder spoke, go into the wood for a coffin
but I was so tired, my head against the dull brocade
of the tapestry, which told me stories of Venus
Mars, this kind of yarns, fragile Renaissance furniture …

and the master builder's speaking skull was itself only
a Mauritanian chess table under my hand lay

I pursed my lips, over the city of the sun, cracks
in the varnish, thoughts – twice buried, and living
I stood, with a lion's head, in the window in the picture.

Bradley Schmidt

HENDRIK JACKSON
Self-Portrait with Aspic

cold snap in april. corners edges floors as if cut, get going
(aslant) in the bustle of the evening city, colours merging on
the verges. just, now in a gesture light miles away from you
dreaming along the *(glassy)* dark bellies, warm half-sleep – dozing

off, then again *(of cars)* a roar *(surges)* rises into the eyes, dive
into *(emerge from)* the intoxicated blue, while people brush by me, whirling
past *(cosmic) (comic)* slowness – separate scenes washed ashore
behind glass, detached, drifting in the air *(blind spots)* heavy and almost

a tangle. no reason to rest any more, dim shall be what was, will
become *(clauses)* fox's fur *(it dawns)* sheep's head. good night. huh.
robbery followed. attempts to erase an impression, wishes hanging
in loops, adding murkiness. murky turnip, as in aspic, addles. doors – falling

Alexander Kappe

DİNÇER GÜÇYETER
from *A Letter, after 35 Years*

wait until I've darned your socks, your little piggies will get wet!
no, grandma, no, my pen pal the sea dragon is waiting for me
he promised to tell me his secret today
please, please I can't miss this miracle
who cares if frost is falling on the fields
if the world is spinning west
or wait, was it the sun? no, not her
she waits in the elevator and whenever she fancies
hits the button, rides up and down
up and down, all cuckoo, like mama fusses!
when she goes down, we're to meet at the castle
of the elephant prince, he's crazy about your
hand pies, grandma, I'll put 3 in my pants pocket
your heart is soft as lamb's wool, it's okay, right?
no? well, I'll only take 3 then
you always say that food in the mouth belongs to all eyes
yes you do, with hand to heart or on the Koran
it wasn't me after all who made up your faith
see you later, sweet Medea, see you later

soak the dried figs in lukewarm milk
on your left breast the Orient will blossom
this flood, this whirl is yours, the day is coming
when the most distant cliffs will hear your voice

Caroline Wilcox Reul

DANIELA SEEL
SAGA

Weather Reports You
Roni Horn

Will, if I reach out my hand, the sea come to me, a stone?

Harsh grace in a dorsal line orients me non-arbitrarily, and so I am here.

And with me a vertigo of emptiness, of a world that takes nothing back.

To interrupt this feeling.

When I say emptiness, do I mean more than empty of humans?

Intoning apocalypse or love, coincidence, cliché with bread soup.

Why should I want to be in the picture anyway?

I have to check the weather. Its disheveled crosscurrent.

All emotions are true.

Everyone here came over water.

Like them I will feel hunger. Dark, desert. Touch.

The sunken forest beneath Cardigan Bay that I looked at from Ty Newydd without seeing it.

What does Hecla have to do with it, Katla, Laki, the Eyjafjallajökull glacier?

Or droughts in Egypt, the French Revolution.

I don't mean this monocausally.

I came through safe third countries, spores on my shoe.

I'm counting on consequences.

Like continents ripping apart and grinding sight in raining ash.

On the green of 600 species of moss.

Entries of the brightest finitude.

Gudridur Thorbjarnardottir, granddaughter of a British slave, traveled, around the year 1000, from Norway to Iceland, Greenland, Vinland, Greenland, Norway, Iceland, Rome, Iceland.

Where she came upon human settlements all over and bore the first European child on American soil, Snorri Thorfinnson.

Which is further than Leifur Eriksson, who for some time was her brother-in-law.

But hardly further than, 500 years later, Enrique Melaka, Malayan slave and translator in the fleet of Magellan.

No survival without seafaring.

No seafaring without conversion of bodies into labour, goods, silence, missions, capital.

Botany also calls mosses pioneer plants.

It says pioneers need dozens of years to grow on fresh lava.

No habitat where water can't flow, soak in.

And dozens more after being uprooted by trampling and grazing.

Meanwhile, introduced Alaskan lupines are to form sediments on deserts left behind by man, cattle, climate.

Degrees of degradation. Sense of possibility.

To briefly find balances in the pull of need and erosion.

Where something gains contours through omission.

I don't mean this as a metaphor.

I mean the kind of fiction that emerges from fact.

My actions translated into selection.

Dreamt of subjection again.

Moments full of inertia.

Where's all this water from?

Fog, foam, clouds, firn, ice, rain, snow –

To enter their density.

That is empty. Endless oscillation within.

Drills me in positioning.

Hypersensitive. Not sensitive enough.

Do birds dream of shores? Or of their flight over oceans?

Ravens climb from my hand.

Their eyes, more than mine, look for lands beyond the sea.

Shane Anderson

BEAST

CAROLIN CALLIES
tweeting is a tiny beast

the breadcrumbs lay, as dry as they are,
three winters now in the hands of trustees
& occasionally they're enough for a loaf.

but let's sugarcoat those crumbs
or pray for them or eat a few
or delete the tweeting from the tape:

later spears tear through the birds, clearly at an advantage
& i'll spare you the sounds that such birds make:
in the end, they merely lisped, as if swooping down from the tape deck.

but did i hoot it or hear it out of their breasts, reddishly widened
or find a crumbful end
or are we now finally brushing beaks from the windowsill?

Paul-Henri Campbell

MONIKA RINCK
what about the animals?

now that it's becoming clear, consider my animal cooked.
futro. the fur. foaming and boiling, the heat of the prongs,
the limp little animal. the neighbours the neighbours
what were their names? it's coming unstuck, coming loose.
timbers work themselves free. a piece of downright
slapdashery, botched from start to finish. it's a fiasco.
the blond roof of straw. how it thrashes about. battles
the wind with the wind, a beating. a rumbling.
anything to salvage or extinguish, perhaps? anything burning?
do the animals need evacuating? plucking from the flames
at the very last moment? no, i hear no screaming.
the animals are fine. which means you can rest at last.

Nicholas Grindell

CHRISTOPH MECKEL
The Child's Report

So dark, there was no longer
anything light on earth.
An animal stood on the road.
The child turned back.

It was the dog
with seventy teeth.
The dog that gulped down stones
like bones.
Hungry for all the stones
and every bone,
great hunger for the child.

The child turned back,
an animal stood on the road.
It was the dog
with ninety teeth,
hungry ninety times for the child.

But the child.
I saw it fly,
fly high up and away.
The dogs devoured
each other in the dark.

Bradley Schmidt

JAN KUHLBRODT
In the House Opposite

In the house opposite, which I can still see through my window despite everything, because last summer, in one big push, I cleaned the windows, a very old couple lives in the house opposite, driving new cars all the time.

I think they are testing the cars, since nobody could afford new cars at such a rate. At least no one who lives in this neighbourhood, unless they moved here to hide their wealth. But then they wouldn't always be driving new cars.

Until a few years ago, this car-testing couple had a dog. When I didn't see it for a while, the piles of books were still manageable. I couldn't imagine them ever growing as much as they have.

There were always three of them: the couple and the dog. None of them walked fast; the dog's lead sagged. He trotted slowly alongside the couple, showing no interest in his surroundings, not stopping every few metres to sniff at something, as I was used to with other dogs, even if it was just the scent of a strange dog, or a piece of clay that an earthworm was living in, an empty yoghurt cup, or a bag like the one I had recently found in the park on one of my increasingly rare walks:

A plastic bag with a breakfast sandwich in it, which had attracted a hedgehog, who had crawled into the bag and become trapped inside. I had to free him, otherwise he would have suffocated.

The dog wouldn't have cared, he would have let the hedgehog die, he would have padded past it like it was an overflowing wastepaper basket. Perhaps the dog's behaviour changed when it was let off the lead in the park nearby and met other dogs. From here, of course, I couldn't see the bit of the park set aside for dog-walking, which was directly behind the park entrance.

I suspect the dog only ever shat under a tree at the edge of the park, smelled his own faeces, was pleased with himself and his performance, and the three of them then turned round to test the next car. Since the dog is no

FRIEDERIKE MAYRÖCKER
a tropical orchid, wild, in his beake

a tropical orchid, wild, in his beake for instance vanilla
no not into the (blacke) spot that's where my glance flew the bird did
not sit in the tree the look-out what have I to fear
a pinion a darke pinion if
its darke pinion swoops to surround me, that's
the first blackbird's cry aching and sweet from the dusty, from the pale
bushes, that is there is hit the mark
the heart I stand there, converse with the bird, reflection
of the heavy sun on the bloody
snow, o what do I desire
my heart my blackbird, hitting the mark in the white
on the fourth of March these melting sounds of Damascene
steel, the quick dripping
heart, the shamed scarred heart, where do they live here ..
: so he addressed me the chap of the cherry tree, leafing
his eye, breath slumbering in the huge trees green-sheathed
before the scruffy storm, plumage of early spring
tell-tale sign of twiggy
limbs in a pair of gazelles' stays, are quivered quoted we in
the parlour's light braid, pleasure virtue and grace
bundled in straw, walking boots the moved glances
of long ago, side-on the blacke eye of the blackbird now
from the threadbare
thicket his blond nape

Nicola Thomas

MONIKA RINCK
orpheus charms beasts of lesser quality

here he sits, at barren altitude, the pines have already moved in close.
as have the oaks, beeches, box trees and the like, the lyre lures.
and just supposing the reason he lost what had almost been
granted was the same as with oedipus: downright arrogance.
look, don't look, going, not going, she's gone. down here: animals.
what doesn't happen by itself is sublimation. there's no two
ways about it. after the plant parade, the animals lie down
at his feet, harmonious and motionless the soft-shelled turtle,
a heath sheep's panoramic flank, a lynx's amputated legs,
the badger's grumpy disposition, snakes come and squint,
she-bears maltreated by saints under the yoke of christendom,
hairy wilderness harnessed in place of oxen, a dismal sanatorium
of insolvency. hunted shadows, shadows hunting animals. animals on ice
and animals on drugs. the healthy animals are doing something else.
a steeplechase. or something with steppe. the healthy animals are watching
their step. dainty hooves dancing the latest steps. not so the crane,
the horses hit by traffic, the inside-out dogs, their fur long since grown
into the cerebellum, moronic hares, and the narco-beast *par excellence:*
the fleeting unicorn. the whole clanking crew. and now: sing one more.
one of your lovely songs, orpheus. and orpheus sang. and sang. and then.
then came the maenads and took things in hand as only they can.

Nicholas Grindell

SEBASTIAN UNGER
The Untied Tamer

Only to sniff shall it step up to him
the roses standing engineer-like, just

so the house on the edge remains in sight
held on this side completely

the Sunday boulder he
pushed before the gaps in the animal kingdom, herculean

set himself aside on toes, that for a life
it stands on tilt, stuck in sesame ajar

and room for an outstretched hand
through starch of linen and white wall

a weight sufficient
to keep him from getting in before the animals get it

see him as one of their kind

Ann Cotten

VERENA STAUFFER
Ling

A fan like that on your back, how that feels, sublime
Is it cold when you flap your wings, how cold it gets
Just not into the sun, just don't melt, folding freezing

lifting, sinking, trying it, it's still a blue morning
an ice-blue morning, not seen one like it for a long time
To walk in it, and slowly flutter, up and down

Well, there you go, it's working, ice is already forming
There goes another over there, how sublimely he glitters, like a ling
She also glitters like a ling, she almost cools a field

This is a heat-based cleaning process for the blue balloon
for the condensed floating dust, for this drying grape
That's how to chase the heat, chase it away, it's always a chase

To the foot of the little apple tree, get close to cool the tree
the little tree is too hot, its leaves rustle hurriedly
It's already getting cooler, soon it'll freeze, now it breaks

Bradley Schmidt

when the ribcage is still
standing, a napkin ring
no one will sew
a shroud for

Ann Cotten

SEASON

FRIEDERIKE MAYRÖCKER
deep blue may, seething

the lovely earth, sobbing out
the blackbird's song, between
the red candles (cowls)
of the trees, the overstory : thun-
dered down cabbage-whites, dwarf
varieties, on the forecourt of the
airport, in beds yellow, violet,
and nodding their heads, so mother
pansy's FATHER'S NAME
while the one bedecked with
gay ribbons at his waist
the garland of box and fir
the May tree, the flame tree, and so on, the coppiced
blossom of the chestnut trees, the deep
red blossom, breaking
at once the long the slumbering
strangeness madness
and thawing all thawing
at last, salt over cheek, fields
of rapeseed blazing, under
the open mouth's
(the swallows)
wound, swift
air arrows,
that is,

for Otto Breicha

Nicola Thomas

MARTINA HEFTER
from *Going to the Woods, Stealing Timber for a Bed*

The fir tree in front of the window is growing, growing, cradles me
in my sleep.
I have the green blood of trees, it roars in me.
The soft wondrous slumbering grass flames
in my eyes, flames, when I look into the garden:
caretaker has sprayed poison again, the weeds lie withered,
dead.
I am still awake. It is night.
What is night to us, the secret ascribed to it, darkening
and sleep, an unaccompanied journey. I like night,
like the garden at night, the shooting grass, the fir thing outside,
the business of fir (tomorrow morning we will know more).
How the birds sleep surrounded by poison.
Night, half-circle with uncertain end. Living with the moon,
night, brighter now in all the LED, the bright sky, the bright faces
of friends that I meet in sleep.
The fir never sleeps, when the photosynthesis stops
its red blood freezes.
I wish I could do that too.

Karen Leeder

MARTINA HEFTER
from *Going to the Woods, Stealing Timber for a Bed*

When I held my seances with the fir tree in front of the balcony
– I know I am too emotional, and this blows unrest into the stars –
the fir tree would say, go inside, sleep, I'll not show you anything now
                                                      [of the coming year.
Year in a box, I unboxed it, a year leapt out,
wide, wild spaces with flights never flown,
lightning in a box, nothing to be illuminated inside.
I was born, newborn, born again or never born in this year
and saw the trams standing still.
I dreamed for a whole year of this year, oh fir tree.
Tell me, how long will it take with this sleep?
You tend it, fire needles, before I fell asleep, I thought
about your pale-green shoots in May, that I cut and steeped in honey,
sealed the jar, drinking the syrup all winter spoon by spoon.
Fir-blood kept me alive that year.
And so, the year passed, the year of sleep passed, as if it were nothing.
When was I torn from the fir, when did I feel the brute force of ideas.
Year. Sleep.
We should long since have thought them anew, differently, shifted them all,
shunted sleep into the cracks of the year, the year into the cracks of sleep.

Karen Leeder

STEFFEN POPP
Fir Trees, the Borderland

Fir trees in the borderland; they bellowed
like a herd, behind barbed wire, boarded up
the customs house festered, tugging
powerlessly at our windbreakers

then open field, a garage looming
under the moon like from a previous world
a miniature box, unreconciled, a sinister
bird triangle shelter above

here loneliness was a railing
spindly, acrobatic, almost a plant

it held us, but we
could not touch it…

Bradley Schmidt

JAYNE-ANN IGEL
Green border

little circuit of the fields, ripe for the frost that arrived bang on time on the first of october, after the twilight of strange dreams (walls meadows blockades, a barrier – not legal but rather one in a terrain that is just the continuation of the meadow i travel, no less green, which astonishes me every time i move along a *green border* marked by the rhythmically arranged sovereign poles: one can count oneself along, and over there, one thinks, space and time are no different, the year combs itself, but then the sum does not seem to add up, for the border-crosser another hour sounds…

Karen Leeder

BIRGIT KREIPE
december is a rhino

december is a rhino.
colossal it stands there in the bony light of grasses and shrubs
ears at attention, the knobby armor
wrinkly. blinking, twinkling under bulging lids.

pollard willows wear a reddish yellow
that burns in the cold, and the weeping willow's thin braids reach
into the empty, gleaming mirrors of gravel-bottomed ponds.

gold dust in the clouds.
everywhere on earth is leaf-strewn: cinnamon snaps. skulls.
water, blank like eyes.

a winter savanna.
the rhino stands utterly still.
its armor encasing its little soul.

is it defending my new freedom?
searching for love?
should we drape fairy lights around the trees?

as it stands there waiting
a thousand sapphire and pink butterflies and birds arrive and
land on the horizon.

the reeds: as though glowing within
and the snowberries are still tottering.
they are old men and women!
they are the audience.

Joel Scott & Lotta Thießen

OSWALD EGGER
Summering

Sermon

SUMMERING. *To seed the fallow with days of passing summer, till, drill, sit in the sun, take in the bloomy hues of field-rud fruits, birch samara, prune the broadleaf of heat-shoots, heather melissa healing-water swaying, sun dogs, their swinging lights and winged-wolf pinions of mayweed bee-balm and zedoary, barometz, the summer-paling spiral-sun of sleep, sheaf ears picture deaf-lights, strip them out, of light*

cut out the lines, eyebright seeding into fleabane, faded now, yellowing, summer-over, a sea as the ship of the jalousie, July, horehound falls, juniper, burning bush. Stook, cut waterways, gather, spread out summer's shucks, "it dusked" and shadow, a soil-rooted dimmit from scraping the earthy colours of the hatched embankment, succory, swirl-the showers stubble-rows in the hay-fire night, spark-stab the furrows, as summer lightning singes, sever, sinter.

ALEXANDRU BULUCZ
Conversations with Tree Bark II

You never bought it when I dreamt of Boris,
of parsnip—*Pastinaken*—fields. Didn't care
what's hidden underneath the taste of dill
in dumplings' cheesy fillings,

what parsley understands about the soul.
You never wondered about Transylvanian apples
or why they're kept in cooling earth,
the mushrooms Majka fried & salted,

the prunes, the schnapps, the great-grandfather,
the stream-side cross of wood. & radish by radish,
onion by onion, you turned a blind eye.
Never have you left white elderflowers

in sun patches to dry for elderflower cordial.
Nor crunched into Andrei's triangular pears
which I picked for us by the roadside,
nor into bitter quinces like Emil the raven.

Never chewed the bread's dark crust,
the jam that Mother brought us,
the white brain of an unripe walnut
whose skin you scrape off with your nails.

No walls defiled with nonsense
by way of the nut's green rind.
Never pretended an apple stem was Earth,
or an apple the sun,

haven't indulged any superstitions,
twisted an apple stem till it tore
to determine the number of turns
round the sun you had left in your orbit.

Lobbed your apple core over & over
onto the compost. In the neighbor's yard,
you never expected the dog bite
in the cherry tree canopy with an ear

as the short shoot of two sweet cherries.
You've never had an itchy back,
a rosehip seed or a Seamus.
You've never attempted

to purge backache from cutting asparagus
with the ache of stinging-nettle lashes,
until nettles stood in for spinach,
& wild ramps for garlic.

Never after the thieving of the leek
the dark grit on your tongue did you talk darkly to God
for lack of water to rinse out the grit.
The angel of Silesia never paid you a visit, like me,

when gathering redeemable bottles.
Why do you keep saying it like me
to the beetles under the bark
in tiny words for tiny footsteps?

Jake Schneider

ANN COTTEN
The Gabion/Ecogravilla

It is hard to walk when walking over these broken fragments
they throw the legs here and there
and with the legs they throw the body keeping the legs together.
This is however still easier
easier work for individualists
– for whom, in the end, all work is absurd –
than to turn the stones over, to sort them, to
acknowledge them and calmly build
paths to be walked on.

Paths to be walked on imply
all kinds of piled up assumptions –
which again are like gravel – about the users of the paths.
The *supposed* users, we wouldn't want to tell anyone what to do.
One step after another is about the most
one can expect another person to do.

A path is a path, and a broad path is a broad path.
A hindrance in classical guerilla warfare, and a help
– clearing the way, if you will –
for mass uprisings as well as the manoeuvring of troops.

Thus come about the groping relations,
where the *nonplusultra* is renewed in every moment
the *nonplusultra* an endless patting down of the other
the other's body and the other's mind.
From outside, they call it gabion, *nonplusultra* is the inner name,
or spirituality, so this text as well,
may it be called from now on not gabion but *nonplusultra*,
for a while, for this symposion.
Because we are
Because we are supposed to
Because we are supposed to imagine everything vividly to the point of it
      melting on our tongue.

Let it come down
                    in a heavy rain
                                    without violence.
You will find yourself standing
                    in heavy rain
                                  lacking necessity
                                          and without violence.
Still the weeds die
                between the stones who cannot die, helpless gabions.

There remain: the factory buildings, the reactors: the reacting poet leaves.
What a turner. Retiring now. The factory stands empty,
no longer a factory. A building. In a hundred years: *ecogravilla*.

Shelter for fresh hipsters lined up for their deflowering.
Pseudo nomads, art clowns, scrolling artists.
The word thrives there like that scented rudeness, wild vermouth.
To tell it all is like the wind driving clouds over Berlin at an insane speed.
As if they were meant not to look too closely.
Long, then, is the way of the backpack-carrying, boot-weary wanderer.
Tedious it is to be human and not yet insane.
Keeping one's legs together with bread and butter and evil-tasting tap water,
this incredible talent of the human race.

A path is a path, and a broad path is a broad path.
A hindrance in classical guerilla warfare, and a help
– clearing the way, if you will –
for mass uprisings as well as the manoeuvring of troops.

Of course, any desert is a hindrance – but they overdo it,
which is also something.
Largely unused potential for masses, furthering the loosening of movements,
the communicability: a broad path is like a telephone.

Riding through Prussia, Napoleon laid curses upon the clinker stones
that paved the *chaussées*, reducing one's bones to a loose sack of gravel.
The roads are deep, dark fen pools inside of a Prussian calculation.

In feudal Japan, disloyalty was prevented,
in a literal sense it could not be organized, there arose no opportunity,
because the regional retainers were required to travel
to the capital with their families every two years.
Gabions, placeholders – can prevent just about anything.

In a kind of natural measure
         – the exact medium between obstruction and suggestion –
the speed of a car regulates itself on a cobblestone road.
The driver leans out her window, at 30 km/hr, dreaming,
         contemplating obsolescence
         contemplating obsolescence
         contemplating obsolescence
         contemplating obsolescence.

Ann Cotten

FRIEDERIKE MAYRÖCKER
from *études*

this branchlet of piano practice ("étude") branchlet practice ("étude") and
how M. Th. K. rushed on ahead through the darkness of campus namely
    at night
that time at night once again not wanting to be intruded upon the light
of morning versus the lark : locks in my eyes I mean the eye
shading shadowing with lark : locks (strands) of the nighttime
lark : locks versus the lily of the valley's bells sounding the morning
bells which I with darkened lark : locks darkening versus
the voice of my beloved echoing in my heart once more eye
of the beloved beckoning versus the lily of the valley's scent baring
shoulder and nape to me (whose glasses slipping to the floor with
a gust / little corner of the sideboard &c.) the pansy's kisses in the morning's
foliage versus the lilac's puffs of breath namely "the

lilac goes to my head .." &c., versus I sleep in the midst of re-
fuse / animals, rhetoric of the evening bells, in the springtime namely in

his CLOGS walks on I hear him walking in his wooden
pattens narcotic florilegium versus rainbow-opalescent
bolt ach death's blink of an eye versus
gullet : endlessly droning writings, il tempo namely daisies time
versus in the light-blue kimono heavens white fluff fancy downy feather of

little cloud already disembodying ...... am thunder-
struck oh murky mignonette green versus repeatedly I scamper at night

to the crucifixion glimpse colossal
facial features in the nighttime vestibule mirror versus
puff of wind (mignon) &c., sm. shako tatterlets of resignation

5/5/11

Donna Stonecipher

MAP

DANIEL FALB
from *CEK*

the glaciers shift everything round, bringing disorder to geological
testimony, leave abrasions on the rock face.
landing pad for university helicopters gives its pulsating signal, in history,
letting me sink down, dawson's faithful beauty on both my eyes,
dawson's sphinx on my mouth.
on the fold belt stretching northeast from lake bonneville, since forever
two inimical universities have taken root, the constellation between them
changing with the icecap.
as chance dictates sometimes one, sometimes the other is on top, on one
of those days dawson strode up the south side of lone peak
and passing the tor noticed a new drilling site
above his own project, from which
since the nebraska glacial great scientific advantage and for him a
 substantial income had been derived.
the ice core is a beautiful and enigmatic artefact.
the foundational myth of the one university and the formational legend
 of the natural phenomena
coincide and the foundational countermyth of the other
university and the formational counter-legend of the natural phenomena
coincide. almost transparent over long stretches of time, the age of
 scientific orogeny
appears at bottom as a still unfrozen
stratum enclosing pungent leaf mould and trembling mildewy moths.
 the great secret guarded by everlasting ice
is ice core extraction. when he approached me
and recognized the university tattoo on my neck, dawson gulped
and tried inconspicuously to button up his shirt, while his pulse beat wildly
in his temples. the natural law behind the phenomena i had been investigating
all my life, dawson,
is you.

Robert Gillett

DİNÇER GÜÇYETER
from *A Letter, after 35 Years*

the camel on the cigarette pack told me the way
my mind is sharper than any map, it said, and I believe it
or at least pretend, so the desert lily isn't angered
our talks, it says, are forever ours, are not for other ears
and even if I laugh again along the way
with the dinosaurs fishing in knee-highs and droopy drawers
am detoured from my sacred path
the wind chime on the handlebars heard everything
may your path always be illuminated, an uncle prayed for me
the prayers of unbelievers are always answered more quickly
and it's true, I fly with crystal breath, the gaze of rabbits everywhere
they stand to my left and right, like a military parade
I come to a halt, drop my bike on the dewy meadow
take a deep breath and utter the magic words the dragon
revealed to me in his last letter, the drawbridge lowers
in the center of the courtyard is the picnic blanket of the 40 thieves
and a watermelon carved into tiny boats
I hear the vines grow, the song of the nightingale
and the words of the uncle, every nightingale is half Turkish
don't be afraid, Dinçer, you've arrived in your ghetto

as cutting as the wind may be
never lower your eyelashes over the shine of your eyes
there were days when you quartered the melon
and munched on the fruit with a child's abandon

Caroline Wilcox Reul

ALEXANDRU BULUCZ
To the Last Meal by Memory Carriage I

from July 7 or 8 to 8 or 9, 2000

It takes us at noon down the riverbank, the Mureș, call it Mieresch, call it
	Marosh.
Which travels from Harghita County, empties into the Tisa. Which empties
	into the Danube, traveling from
outside Rakhiv. Which travels from the Black Forest, hits the Black of the
	Seas.

How selfless rivers really are when a river mouth's a muzzle.

We ask the roadside berries about water tables. They hold a consultation
with a tapeworm. Who curls back up into the red fox. Who in turn believes
the horses were still hauling yesterday. Who snort at us: that's your answer.

How selfless rivers really are when they've had it up to here.

We'd dunk the ćevapčići, hot, in mustard & then proceed to the tripe soup.
Cattle bleat at us, it doesn't do to nitpick so soon before the border business.
We keep fishing out vinegared rumens & heaving memory up from brew
chambers.

Check out the blotch on Gorbachev's head: a Latvian map rotating clockwise!

Jake Schneider

ALEXANDRU BULUCZ
Crișcior Straw Road

The coachman, the lad with the stubbly beard, was a Rom
whose two draft horses, Peter & Werner, were sniffing their wealth,
while I headed in debt down the bumpy straw road,
in a dream to the grange, as the hills all around raised their arms
to the skies in a plea for the Lord's urgent aid.

Oh how mortally misty is luck! What an Eden to hear
the first cackles & crowing of cocks, at which Majka
pries off the tough kernels from cobs in the glinting tin pail
before flinging her hand right to left as she scatters
gold teeth for the beaks of the toothless ones.

Swift, after breaking a serious sweat, to the fish
in the brook, down the crest of the slope to the salt lick,
forgetting what whetstones would shout from their watery
pouches on hips that twist steely through June's early grass:

"Sharpened the blade of the axe from the oak chopping-block,
as it struck at the blood-seeping wounds" & the cocks doodle-dooed
for industrious reapers, the traveling Rom in the evening
& plenty polenta that glistened quite bright in its dish.

Jake Schneider

ANN COTTEN
ICE

A monkey cage this buffet car, and still
the nicer paneling than in the open carriage
filled up with over 80 human larvae eating rolls
with gooey stuff and sad lettuce in them, and talking.

To enter into this, and not to breathe,
and not to think, but hear the Teflon-talk,
and undead wrappers, fucking personal space
behind your ear, and more words, excel silence.

We're a bit short of power,
says the cute conductor
with the many earrings.

Beastly German men surround
the sales counter that opened
in Ulm.

Ann Cotten

STEFFEN POPP
After the Rifle Fire II

The rich land erects trees and remains silent
the water city is almost the sea
a herb one could use against wasteness on the river
the heart slowly starts; the heart, the heart.

The meadows heavy with dew, cubes of light
around your feet the grass, hesitant hydra
the talk of the birds is in the throat of the night
but no animal can sing for your sleep.

Veins run through the woods like skin
the land says *stand*, the earth wanders
an opportunity for you to lift your head
but it is so much and only wants to breathe.

The darkness sucks in space, feels like wood
not an element made of stars, just fire
unaccompanied, you cross the river, the tracks
and over the open field, which changes you.

Bradley Schmidt

HENDRIK JACKSON
protection from stalking – as i imagine it

bin laden goes into the mountains, admirable & bearded he goes
across the mountains in the second german tv channel and in all of them.
what is, from here, the other side of the capitalist coin:
eagle or eichmann, goethe or lenz? wrong: *(baudrillard)*

gosh. the media call him: "hole hello? halo?" holla!
"yeah, hell here, got a video". cheerful europeans.
the devil invades the detail. the network is leaking! is there still
spit space under the *(networked)* tongue of the prophet?

a bogof, how confusing: hussein and al-qaeda.
information leaks out: they have given up everything *(in eden)*,
even their integrity, keyword: timing, good handling.
the lion of münster agrees: fear god, not man.

controversial issue. what causes more devastation? put a full
stop here, treat yourselves to something factual, that is: holograms.
at night: abstractions on top of that *(the beard!)*. left spitting.
take the dynamite belt, see how lovely the hand sweats.

whether one ascends like you to be the shining light of reflection,
one evening in the quiet club, goes all gangster
in the party crowd *(of the apocalypse)*, issues fuzzy statements
or expects to generate millions of dollars, thousands of deaths

or inspires new fictions – rising oil prices, your empty wallet
(fact) – that's the same thing, you numbskulls. who would still
plant geraniums *(when people are swaying as one in the squares)*?
stop imagining now, look for the stone

Alexander Kappe

CHRISTOPH MECKEL
Ashen Gold Ash

– where the vehicle passed by
quickly disappeared, a sound stayed in the air
we looked for traces in the light, in the shadows
perhaps something had been peeled off, fallen out
stuck to the side of the road, to trees and stones,
clouds, raindrops, birds,
shoes and the eyes of children, ashen gold ash –

Bradley Schmidt

STEFFEN POPP
Auratic Agrology

I

Imperceptibly cultivating a style, wind from the Northwest
and the garage door compose a flowing rectangle

the emotional project, strung out
it hangs before us, in the air, breathing laboriously

we seek to bind love's structures
in conversation, in the long forest-walks
through fog.

II

The heart foams heavily in its gazebo of pain
wild vines, screams, dry roses, silence

darkness spreads geometrically in quiet rows
in the island's hem of water lilies, floating pond scum
and forests are and
premises, within which you vanish

the area, naturally artificial, correctly incubated
the loneliness of your mud boots, pragmatic
under your white knees

and in the evening can we not hear, behind the drunken roar
of lost witnesses, your swans in the biosphere, singing.

III

Always in shades of tiredness
snowed in, in mountains, in plains, in one's own body
to encounter—a

       distant shore, overgrown with light,
floating in self-invented fog…

Odd correspondence with narcissi, saxifrage
this special technique was called "living",
               "home"

instead we wanted to go deeper into the distilleries of tenderness
to never end this undistracted Yes

words, their sorrow, penguin tracks on the pack ice
—to look at you walking, breathing, to contemplate
your childish fists in sleep…

IV

Speaking exhausts the community of pain
future settles on thought like a mold, like fire

in the rotunda, a red horse standing there, made from copper
the blood in your fingers, the party lights
ring the trees like a wilted piano.

To walk around, restless, striking a few keys
sometimes the music lures something out

the instant in the play of twigs
a longing, carved out of cheap stone lovers announce the night

cold fusion, centaur

whoever steps within range of trees is alone.

Christian Hawkey

JAYNE-ANN IGEL
The blue blood of the rivers' courses

I remember how we copied them from the map using tracing paper in our local history class – All the local occupations, to give our home, the city, this body of land, a shape, *my district*, the outline of which on the map looked like a molar, a tooth that any dentist would have deemed impacted and would soon have to be removed…

Laid down within was the vein-work of rivers, only blue on the map, which was why i kept having to draw them again, without being asked – They fascinated me, these lines, some filigree, like hairline cracks, like the boundary lines that seemed to follow the irregularities of the earth, creating a network of pockets and exclusions, in which every point had a meaning…

Karen Leeder

YEVGENIY BREYGER
from *Peace without War*

do you smell the plastic breath of the dead? do you hear
the talks between arms like branches, fingers like twigs
the gestures of bone fractures, how they act coyly at the core
as images of the ONE g'd, the ONE 'trauma
oh, but yes, but of course dear god, oh you dear bone god, bone-
crack, music from the innards, the very long missed ones
that emerge from memory like cormorants, clay people
spoken with the words of language – ask the idol
to keep watch for you, when you take a deep breath
one MOMENT of not paying attention and "ll be
burning on the mattress, but it can also be different
can turn out well and suddenly a work would arise
dead as an official's eyes, and YET
work ... (smallest idea ever conceived)
imagined just for once: the president stands in the hole
deciphers CRUELTY as IM-
perative out of the hole and your cheeks glow and caimans

burn their scaly tails into sandbanks
where everything wears out, disintegrates into particles of dirt
and someone giggles next to you that today is his birthday
it is the sixth day of creation, i am lenient
write my parents *how's things* in the chat. wait a minute
wait a minute? "d love to start a speech
by saying where "m going, but "m just stopping off, like any human being
bow-legged and strange
take me, g'd, my moments are long like 1000 trains
pull me, g'd, out of the misery
pave the paths of my loved ones with addiction and substitutes
cut into your third eye with a penknife
DEAR g'od, oh god, let your brain be made of mud
that you may understand me
that you may carry my loved ones through dazzling thought
and darkness – disguised as light
and music on joints, peace, without war

Alexander Kappe

TOM SCHULZ
Circle Train

in search of half a cent,
the punks stood by the moving
stairs, back then we didn't know that
what we scrawled on the benches in crayon
was nothing but another invention of
industry, the TV sets went black
and white: Dynamo Moscow beat Torpedo Moscow
CSKA Moscow in a tie, you wore
an eye patch and were not a music pirate
I had tattooed my tongue with
there is no reason why, the public
transport smelled like disinformed detergents,
there were only productive forces and class
less bras with the salute of the *Free
German Youth*, the drums gave a crash
like the fall of the Roman empire
in a set by *Müllstation* from Frankfurt an der Oder
some things remain forever
young like a handful of sherbet

the punks hanging around the lift for
the disabled in search of lost time,
time killing the money without which
nobody can buy their way out, the ticket
inspectors smell like cheap hair tonic when
after "instruction on the legal consequences"
someone gets removed from the misallocation list

we've passed them all, left before
right, when the circle train sings
*and the alcoholics' orchestra
rehearses the latest aria*
and with political slivovitz on channel sixteen
the satellites crack their livers to smithereens

Gerald Fiebig

MACHINE

ULRIKE ALMUT SANDIG
from 'Songs of the Radio Tower'

ACT 1   *Min 0:00 Film starts*
                                            Shadows and shadows and – night!
                                            without a voice I cannot say
                                            let there be –

but in the beginning was the water.   *Min 1:01 Water*
from the water comes all that speaks.

we always want back to the water
can't you hear it roaring behind you?

keep turning, metallic eternity thing   *Min 1:21 abstract cuts*
become a wave on the Bohemian shore   *with turning movement*

roll across the Saxon steppes full
of meadows, pine trees, stones in the track bed.

later the loose piles of gravel, but still
the same soft sand underneath us.

we were born of the water
in trains we came rolling back.

❄

later still we were children   *Min 4:57 Town-hall clock*
and already no two of us alike

that you are a twin, only occurs
to you as someone else performs

the old Welcome and Farewell
in the Palace of Tears again

just look how they're acting out
the history teacher mutters

such a spectacle at Friedrichstraße!
and who is shut up here anyway

us or them? *were i but a little bird*
with my two little wings

you carry your twin in your voice box   *Min 5:48 grey sky,*
you cry out in two dialects: *metal scaffolding*

❄

down with you, you party spooks   *Min 6:49 Shop-window mannequins*
disappearing into the underground station

what's that tumbling across the street   *Min 6:59 blowing paper*
time travellers between the years?

swarms of weary tourists?
ghostly apparition in old black-and-white   *Min 7:27 black-and-white cat*
films that no one knows anyway?

keep up, you Madonna-runners   *Min 07:38 tired passers-by*
eyes front past the explosion of colours   *overacting*
past the giantesses on the posters   *bizarre luggage*
     past the Litfaßsäule

my girl. i fly to you   *Min 7:50 pigeons*
because it can be so!

once again an epoch   *Min 8:28 train leaves the station*
takes its mechanical course.

Karen Leeder

DANIEL FALB
from *the clearance of these parks*

native vegetation a natural resource, the very gesture – ethnic
in this accelerating humanity go-round and you,
                          the face on which you're riding.
the miss-pageant report started right there.

    before remodeling provisionally migrants were
housed in the hall, and now again.
    we had to go, you looked simply exquisite, or
i did. the international face was surely

    a gateway to the world, but who could keep on watching.
and in the open spaces of these reserves, the *party*,
we stood knee-deep in the grass, and i didn't know
                                      where to look.

Brian Currid

SONJA VOM BROCKE
Sonar's Supper of Wrath

"I am encased in a shell – and they are juggling!"

you pile the bats into clumps of rage
chewing on leather tunics, work muscles
cram yourself into the heart
and nerve strangulators, a heart-nerve strangulator
machine gender, calibrated.

Of course calibrated! And it's abandoned by all reason
with the mini-jugglers in the courtyard of death
you feed in tassels, dried hermaphrodites, crust –

you bite into foam. Oh.
Nibble it off . . .

Catherine Hales

CHRISTOPH MECKEL
Little Windmill

– Windmill, the half-grown, little one
does not want to spin, no wind can help
suffers from rust in its spine
needs rest, what I meant to say,
I put up another one
over the door that leads to the endlessness
of your junk room
pink as a hoodlum's tie
rustles and chirps, the wind is in love –

Bradley Schmidt

GEORG LESS
fifth vertebra / we beleaguered

raced, pitched tents above cities, hardened with a thousand-
odd pegs the land, sleep went up in smoke
under the onslaught of working days when we harvested wreaths from
      the edge

echo of new alloys, someone was disturbed, since one night
the whole enemy tribe, an echoing
grove of worn-out faces, stood a thousand-
odd strong below us, thereupon we grasped our isolation
a multitude in rage

the fifth horse, habitude, followed riderless, we raced
round what was established, in orbits of destructive
drifters and leaned softly into the curves seeking
sleep on nearby planets, straight roads are not open to us

Chris Fenwick

SABINE SCHO
from *The Origin of Values*

In lieu of a prologue, something more like an undertow that initially leads away from the subject at hand

It's not a trivial topic to ask about fiefdom. Earthly possession.
Who assigns it? Who takes it? Who uses it and how? Who digs in their heels?

Leased land, for example? Which illustrious volume, the Bible, for example, leaves here illustrated?

It isn't trivial to ask: who set foot first? Who measured,
paced, fenced off? High house. No hill, a residence. Yours.
Watching the corn ripen and splice from here? How does that work?

Farm machines as big as *New Holland* harvest the planting stripes. Separate wheat from the chiffchaff. Birds of prey cry until scorching
shines in the face, but to whom? Branded by belonging, as if the sweat vassal! Yes, as if.

It can't be fully imagined. Considered as a surface. Take the planet
from a Soyuz, embrace it with your hands, dribbling fissures from its
rugged shores, rebuffing it how? Which is shouldered by
whom? And carried where? How far?

It isn't trivial to dig, or to strip something away, to rip holes, or to
plant. Soy, yes, that's it! Who knows if where something is, there was not
      something else
before? And where nothing was another nothing, right? Ibirapuera.

Determine what should grow, for better or for worth. Trade everything
that withers on the stock exchange. Who knows whether every bulb will
      become a tulip,
a toucan escapes from every egg. As colourful as egg paints.

An iron ore plant in the *rich mines* of Brumadinho turned the landscape
    rust red.
The land now wears a different colour: mud, contaminated. The treasures
    are not always out
in the open, and a colour system vowed
that it would colour every disaster by name.

Scabs on maps, scratching yourself when it itches. Standing by the geysers
there the world blows bubbles. A kingdom for a plaster and a falcon
for the queen. Formed by failure, that makes sense.

A cauliflower-like structure of biofilms thanks its predators that are not
yet born. Grows 0.3 millimetres higher every
year. Could take a while until a mutt lifts its leg against it.

Stromatolite meets stray dog. Now I could mark here, where a territory

begins.

Bradley Schmidt

SEBASTIAN UNGER
Theory of Signs (B. F. Electrics)

This sudden tendency of the clouds to be *definitive*
eye holes, brows above (with the trowel of curiosity)
in each case the spot that points to itself!
the roof not yet struck by lightning, an assertion
to which the birds return

As he now steers the wire-reinforced kite into the clouds
something like a pointing rage flowed through hollow bones
in the pointing stick or in blood
of a light-footed deixis: weren't fingers also toes?
wasn't pointing
the lightning of ideas diverted skyward?

What kind of pointing should that be: the farewell shape of hands
a soft globe dons dripping landscapes
with an x-ray grip
meridians, however
deep-rooted, lifelines, as the sign finally struck

Alexander Kappe

DAGMARA KRAUS
be brave, moon
(for a child)

*i don't understand how people
can write poems about the moon…*
            zbigniew herbert

            pink pipsqueak: moonspy, dwarf
        mark of midnight—fizzdapple, a sun-
disputing tricky dick, faintly lit and

            distant. a clicker, ice-stone, you stray glossy
        over the huge arc; loose eyelet, orphaned
on the starched collar of stark night

            —drift-sand? blaze? didn't david work you,
        with his sling, high into the heavens'
braid, and steal orion's fame?

            i portioned out the nightcrêpe, made
        myself a shift of it; with the brooch,
your halo, gathering the universe's fabric—

            how the gamma-owls will envy… and
        the broke goliath whose brow you chalk,
lodestar, now has twice no clout

Joshua Daniel Edwin

DANIEL FALB
from *CEK*

geodesic domes, surrounded by undergrass, landed... waterfalls and
    nurturing
wells in soilless hydroponics. i no longer see

the eyes that once saw the kaiser...... kindergarten, shredded tissue, pieces of
the socius hanging down, cultivated within days like grass stems. and

countless, still rolled up dimensions of parliament sucked in matter... while
to themselves they cried quietly. unroll the blossoming meadow.

their roots rinsed in a sheet of rocky mountain spring water: the friendship
networks. persian carpet and trailer park, replaced over night by replicas. the

primary method of reproduction stretches overall until the horizon......
    an mca.
that was the history of aids from 1900–1950.

Christian Hawkey

SABINE SCHO
Aircraft Cleared for Take-Off

on a curved little patch
up into the air 'as if an angel is
pushing them along'

upliftings: 'how they fly!'

wedding-formations in the frenzy
of light

dreamers at the acoustic-
baffle, one wing with scratched-
on graffiti, wonky stucco-
work in the domed hall

having stormed the skies
'the geometricians took
the countries from us and
the astronomers the heavens
long ago'

robbed of antennae
carried away by the sea
of air 'fallen aeroplanes'

Karen Leeder

LORE

SONJA VOM BROCKE
Lore

The doctor phantom on the terrace. If you slip out of your shoes now
will the serpent protect you or attack you?
And what now.   No
you have no idea. You pay for your fries and stumble
blow into the Pan neck, crunch
and think of Gregor, Saskia or Ev
with her full head of hair you can see is exhausting.
She bears her child as to the manner born, with a brooch for bling.
A breeze wafting to her of mallow and tap dancing and the guy (sporty
            type guy)
has big, strong toes and takes a bite from an apple.

While you are creeping in, once again gaming away your breasts
(modulate) and petrifying to a bust. In which a tenacious tendon, a – noble –
a – hollow –
            spacious cult house of the Abelam.

Does the serpent protect you now, or does it attack you?

Catherine Hales

BIRGIT KREIPE
witch k

once upon a time:
fairy tales of fire
cinnamon, lime, pink:
autumnal pyromancy
in the form of swirling wind.
the leaves blowing up to the fourth floor.

here lives ms. kreipe, rattled the door,
a witch. dreams of teeth
as warm as tongues and blood.
the door tattled on. *when she speaks*
red things fall to the floor
nobody who enters here
enters the same river twice.

as i came in something was spinning
around the room, something like a leather jacket.
a rocker gang keeping its own company
it delved through drawers
albums, diaries…
hurry up, i warned,
the colours of everything are fading fast.

we could pack all this here up in black
and talk about depression,
some old biddy-box suggested.
it was stuffed with tarot cards.
i'd never taken any notice of that before.

it became a pigeon-beat
spoke of nutcrackers, meaning the floor.
heard voices, but it was just the talking clock.
had nothing to say, that was all.

right at the bottom, crocodiles,
i said.
it turned up its collar.

people, i thought, you have no idea
when i say *wind*
you're gone.

Catherine Hales

STEFFEN POPP
Footnotes from the Margins of Antiquity

You contemplate the plain, ashes
a grey tone in the layers means
"Rome", a rust coloured pocket "Bonn"

a hetaera's amulet
beneath the warmth which spreads like a yearning
from your hand into the metal

the war elephant's tusk touches you
with its fractures, cracks

ride out, it says, search for the heart
I was devoted to, that has been beating for you
for a long time.

Bradley Schmidt

THOMAS KLING
serner, carlsbad

where in announced surroundings
the censorship began its babbling

central granite massifs.
salted snow. I didn't

know anything, seventy-two
about a House Edelweiss where

mattkaiser chasm or ochre-
toned or other sort of memoirs

"speak up"
in karlovy vary

… the (midday?) sun, weakened,
was announced in mirrors; where

the becherovka rang in cut-glass
Beakers and speech on the marble

gleam. carlsbad-sounds:
"oh speak up" in pickled

snow, and "every substantive a
return ticket"   SERNER

who went on the trip from prague
group ticket to the gas.

Andrew Duncan

THOMAS KLING
Ghosts

Ghosts in 1913 the rivers and mountains on Papua New Guinea
have long since been named after Hohenzollerns.

the head of the alien whirrs and delivers. for new
faraway things new names as languages

mix. in the mouth which savours the alien the new
like copra or cassowary. that goes with the helmet. so

new masks from the swamp-islands steam
on the sublime tongue of the Westland. the

palates billow crackle with a fresh wind from overseas. berlin –
the tongue – raises itself as a fresh island of the dead out

of the fever swamp of the March. the island clicks its tongue already
words are coming out of the faraway. tropical fruits fall

from the town's mouth. whose new tongue is
so chatty. somehow other: suddenly everyone

is speaking like the Papua, court language Iatmul. the mouth as oversea, as appearance. so the Sepik flows and runs into the Rhine.

Andrew Duncan

BIRGIT KREIPE
training session with the white man

the dancing of glances in the air
blue electric eels

completely sufficient
for the assumption of sovereignty.

i clambered silently across stairways
bright as piano keys, sky-high

and descended the same
steps again, bright as

crackling bones, honed
to a shine, deep as history.

in a cellar a light sat imprisoned.
the white man was bright as phosphorus

i thought i was levitating – not unpleasant –
and if the sea was very cold

the hospital was perhaps a fisher-of-men-
net and the old idea:

if i can only swim far enough away
then i can reach my own coast

i'd be levelled, perhaps i'd have
a substitute sea

with a white lifeguard, my head
would swim whole circuits

my mouth full of joined-together words
neuroleptic sweet things

and i'd be in my thoughts: would be

an even flickering
in the electroencephalogram

Catherine Hales

ULF STOLTERFOHT
the forty-five bloodjesus legends

(1)

1| the life of bloodjesus suggests that he was a saint.
the "rule" is testimony to his poetry. the church, however, presents
him as a phenomenon. which is also borne out by these legends.
the numerous horde of his followers underlines his virtue as
a holy man, poet and father. on the whole he was a devout old dog.

2| bloodjesus comes from an aristocratic family near worms. he is sent
to houston to study philology. passionate in his love for christ, he digs
deep, but conscientiously knows very little. for want of a classical
education he, together with the lady who's providing for him,
leaves his course and houston, heading roughly to the north-east.

3| he reaches oklahoma city and stays because the people there
give him alms. one day his provider borrows a sieve, but it breaks,
she turns sadly to bloodjesus. he takes the pieces, takes himself
off to pray. the sieve is as good as new again. the people find out
about the matter and hang the sieve up in their church.

4| but bloodjesus wants no praise, so he leaves both district and provider. he makes his way towards the solitude of waco. on the way
he meets the monk who asks him this and that. when the monk
clearly recognises his terrible intent, he takes the habit, which
is just the same as consecration to god. that pleased bloodjesus.

5| he takes refuge in the narrow, bare grotto, staying there for years, unknown to anyone except the monk. he lets food down to him in a wastepaper basket and rings a bell as a signal. but satan grudges bloodjesus the food, so he breaks the little bell with a sharp stone.
but that doesn't bother the monk – he just keeps on helping him.

(2)

6| the monk dies at some point. at easter god appears to a
priest and lets him know in no uncertain terms that his
servant bloodjesus is suffering from hunger. the priest goes to
the place he's told; when he finally finds the holy man he tells him
in a roundabout way that it's easter. then they eat together.

7| just a short while later a few shepherds discover bloodjesus.
he's bedecked with leathers and has long hair so they take him
for a wild beast. but then they recognise the man of god in him
and learn to like him. in return for food they get loan words
from him that they keep in their hearts. a good exchange.

8| one day the devil flutters about his head as a blackbird.
bloodjesus drives him off with the sign of the cross. then he's
overcome by temptation of the flesh. he almost gives in, has already
got his kit off, but instead hurls himself into a bed of nettles and thorns
in which he rolls around. soul's salvation saved by torn flesh.

9| monks from a nearby monastery want him as their abbot;
once they realise that he won't put up with their shenanigans, a
decision is made: to get rid of him with poisoned wine! before the
first sip he again makes the sign of the cross – the chalice
shatters. he begs forgiveness and goes back to his grotto.

10| he's famous now. a lot of people follow his example. he
founds twelve monasteries, appoints an abbot in each of them
and names the monks. aristocrats come to him to offer him
their offspring: callahan brings young moro and the tempered thatcher
entrusts him with the lad superbus. let's see what happens.

(3)

11| one monk is unable to pray with the others any longer. his abbot
ticks him off repeatedly, but it does no good. he asks bloodjesus for
advice, who sees at once that some black devil has him in
its grip. moro can see it too. bloodjesus sets about chastising it
with a stick. since then things have turned around with him for the better.

12| three monasteries, built on rocks, have no water within reach, may they be moved! at night bloodjesus and superbus climb up the mountain, pray and place three stones. the monks are told to dig in these spots and behold, they go thence, set to with spades and soon water in plenty is bubbling forth.

13| the next day a goth is clearing a patch of land with a sickle. the sickle blade falls into the lake. the trembling goth tells moro, who informs bloodjesus, and he goes to the lake, picks up the handle and hurls it into the water. then sickle blade and handle are reunited – and the goth can calmly carry on his work.

14| once, when the boy superbus is scooping water with a pail, he falls into the pond. in his cell bloodjesus senses what has happened, calls moro and orders him to help. so moro goes there, and though he believes he's still walking on solid ground, he's actually walking on water. and thus he grabs superbus by the scruff of his neck and brings the child to shore unharmed.

15| bancroft tries to subvert the souls of the disciples. he has seven maidens dance outside the monastery. the aim is seduction. the good bloodjesus is as concerned about moro as about superbus and decrees a change of residence. he issues a rule for the disciplinary system of the monasteries and departs to destinations unknown. we're guessing carmel.

(4)

16| bancroft is punished right away. the terrace of his house gives way and he's squashed to a pulp. then moro wants to acquaint bloodjesus with what has happened, runs after him and tells him all. the holy man is saddened at the death of his rival, but even more at the gloating of his disciple moro. a small penance is imposed.

17| when bloodjesus reaches mount carmel, a temple has already been raised there. he smashes the statue of the false god, tips over the altar and valiantly burns down a grove of trees. his old evil enemy, however, pesters him in every way he can and constantly mocks him with "bloodjesus? you're not bloodjesus!". the worthy father alone remains unfazed.

18| now for something really odd: the monks build walls
but a huge rock stands in their way. despite every effort it will not shift.
the devil must be dwelling in that hunk of rock. bloodjesus is informed.
he hurries immediately to the scene and prays as is his wont. now
the rock is suddenly quite light. the work can carry on.

19| as they are digging the monks discover a bronze idol, which they
casually toss into the kitchen. a fire breaks out there straight away.
it fumes as though the whole building were on fire. water is unable
to put it out. bloodjesus gets to the pandemonium and sees at once:
the fire is fake, just an illusion! it vanishes with prayer.

20| the devil plays even more tricks. where they're building he makes
the walls fall down and they bury a little monk beneath them. bloodjesus
has the little monk taken to his cell, which is wise. he prays really hard
and a miracle occurs. the little monk seems healed and goes
back to his work (this legend is disputed and unverified to this day.)

(5)

21| once two monks are detained for longer than expected outside
the monastery. so they stay with a woman and eat with her in con-
travention of the rule. it's late when they come home. bloodjesus wants
to know where they ate. "nowhere", they reply. then he enumerates for
them all that they have eaten and drunk. the pair are sincerely mortified.

22| a devout, sober man was in the habit of meeting bloodjesus every
year. on the way there another wanderer suggests breaking his fast.
he resists twice; the third time he tucks in with gusto. when he arrives
at the monastery, bloodjesus tells him in no uncertain terms of his
transgression. the man falls to his knees and begs forgiveness.

23| the sheriff gives the deputy his own boots and sends him off
in them to bloodjesus, just to see if the holy man really possesses
the gift of clairvoyance. as soon as bloodjesus sees him he starts
yelling, "take those boots off – they're not yours, they don't
belong to you!" the deputy is shocked and dismayed.

24| so the sheriff himself sets off to see bloodjesus. before he
approaches, he kisses the ground. bloodjesus helps him up. but do
not be deceived! then he reproaches him for all his misdeeds and
iniquities and tells him how he will end up. the sheriff is astounded.
he does a quick act of worship then leaves with clearly milder feelings.

25| fitzroy, bishop of arizona, visited the holy man often. once
they talk about the invasion of tucson by the huns. bloodje-
sus points out that the town will not be destroyed by bar-
barians but by lightning and storms. the bishop strongly
doubts this. but that's exactly what later came to pass.

(6)

26| a priest from el paso is being tormented by the devil. he's
taken to consecrated laredo, but it's all in vain. only bloodjesus
can manage to drive out satan. then he urges him most insistently
to spurn the flesh of the jay. after a while, however, the priest
has another taste of it. the devil vexes him to death.

27| the monk konradin, a turncoat iroquois, sees that blood-
jesus is weeping and asks him why. because the monastery and all
that's been laid out for the brothers must be written off:
the mohicans are going to destroy it. but he, bloodjesus, will make it
so that only the walls fall down and the brothers stay unharmed.

28| young peabody sets off from corpus christi bringing two
bottles of whisky for bloodjesus. when he's only half-way there he drinks
one himself. when he hands over the second bottle, bloodjesus tilts it
and a snake slithers out. it tells him that the other one is missing.
nothing can stay hidden from bloodjesus. everything comes to light.

29| a worshipper accepts a few coverlets from sinful nuns during the
sermon and hides them from the master. he notices at once of course
and tells the worshipper so. but he is most unwilling to part with
them. you should see the holy man now: his wrath is great and he
disowns the whole caboodle. then the worshipper caves in.

30| billy, a novice, who holds the oil lamp during the meal to light up bloodjesus, thinks to himself in secret: who the hell does this man think he is that i have to hold this lamp for him. then the saint reads off his thoughts to him exactly one by one and asks him to leave. when the others ask him what has happened, he unbosoms and admits it all.

(7)

31| in pasadena there is great famine: five loaves of bread for the whole city! bloodjesus bids the people have courage and says, "verily your situation today is needy, but tomorrow you will have everything in plenty!" the next day there are two hundred sacks of flour outside the city gates. still not clear who put them there.

32| bloodjesus sends a few men to abilene to set up a house of prayer. "go! i'll be coming along soon with the plans." but he does not come, instead he sends them instructions in a dream. the men are annoyed and go back home to complain to him. he replies and says, "did i not appear to you? now do what i told you in your dream!"

33| two nuns are castigating a servant; he turns to bloodjesus, who has him pass the message on that they should tame their tongues, or else they'd be excommunicated. shortly afterwards they die. the deacon refuses to bury them. then some sanctimonious lady sees them flying around the churchyard as ghosts. bloodjesus permits their laying to rest.

34| once a monk leaves the monastery without permission. his path takes him to palestine, where he falls ill and stays. after his burial, his grave twice hurls him out again. bloodjesus recommends laying a host wafer on the dead man's chest. and what do you think happens? the earth no longer spits him out. it keeps hold of him.

35| a young man who is suffering from elephantiasis is brought to see bloodjesus, who heals him and gives him into the hands of his father. another man has been poisoned out of jealousy. he survives, but his body is covered in sores that look like leprosy. bloodjesus is able to heal this man, too. his skin is whiter than snow.

(8)

36| a man comes up to bloodjesus to complain about being relentlessly downcast on account of being owed twelve months' pay. "come back in three days, what you're asking for is not here today." bloodjesus prays. when the man comes back there is thirteen months' pay on the shrine, twelve months for the creditor and a month's pay to cover his expenses.

37| hunger again! and only half a bottle of oil is left. deacon hume asks at the monastery for more, but the master of the feast refuses to give it to him. enter bloodjesus. he hurls the bottle against the rocks, but behold! it doesn't shatter. on the contrary, the top starts lifting up and oil starts pouring out because it's overfull.

38| the devil pretends to be a medic and examines the monks. the holy man finds one who's already been quite a bit possessed. possession occurred when he was drawing water from the well. when bloodjesus sees how the poor man is suffering, he administers him a good clip round the ear, which immediately drives out the unspeakable one. (perhaps this legend lacks a little drive.)

39| a greedy goth named lloyd is torturing a peasant, whereupon he admits to him the wealth of his master. the goth ties up the peasant so that he can take him to the latter. with a single glance bloodjesus unties the rope. the goth hurls himself at the holy man's feet. bloodjeses gives lloyd something to eat and gives him a proper ticking off for his cruelty.

40| the monks are tilling the fields. a farmer goes to the monastery and lays his dead child before the door. the holy man drops to his knees beside the child's body and prays, his arms arced skyward. soon it works, the child awakes. bloodjesus proudly presents it to the father. very shortly after this the monks come back from working in the fields.

(9)

41| at their last encounter, scholastica asks her brother bloodjesus to stay in waco to give tidings of the coming kingdom of heaven. he refuses because he's not permitted to spend the night away from the monastery. scholastica cries and prays to god. now suddenly a storm breaks out and bloodjesus sees himself compelled to stay.

42| after three days give or take bloodjesus sees his sister's soul in
the form of a dove ascending to heaven. he rejoices at this triumph
and thanks god with hymnic songs. then along come several monks
and take her body on their shoulders to lay her in the same
tomb that's already been earmarked for bloodjesus.

43| one night bloodjesus sees from his window how the whole world
seems to be joined with a ray of the sun. it is the soul of creed,
bishop of wichita falls, going to god in flames. the master straightway
sends a man there and he finds out that creed really did
die that self-same night. the apparition did not lie.

44| one more occurrence. a madwoman is going about in the mountains
day and night. one day she finds her way into the grotto of bloodjesus
where she spends the night. at daybreak she slips away from there,
mentally fit. it was the vestiges of the master that performed this thing.
holy trinity intercede for us that we may erect his kingdom here on earth.

45| bloodjesus himself however embarks on the last ship going from
glencove to bremerhaven. there he takes the night train to berlin,
then from gesundbrunnen directly to grossgoerschenstrasse, where
he leaves the s-bahn and walks to bautzener strasse. we've been
waiting for him here. welcome, lord bloodjesus, to our new jerusalem!

Catherine Hales

HOME

ULJANA WOLF
stationary

what is a domicile? a domicile is a star-
crossed ten of clubs. what is a crossing?

in the flubbed dialect of these forests
a crossing is the word tree. and why

do homelands play cards in the air? no one
ever saw the homelands go home. a tree

in the forest of neighboring languages
is a club in this suit. out of its wood

someone makes crosses on a map.
the countries fill in their domicile and

put the stationery back into its pencil
case. what is stationary? put it back.

with nelly sachs

Sophie Seita

TOM SCHULZ
The Working Class Queues up at Lidl in the Evening

Orlando with game:
a ragout of tragic roles.

Dogs with four eyes
scrounge for butt-ends and booze.

I negate that man is a commodity.

Between the special offers:
birds as spiders.
Germany must give itself a
hawk. A spotted woodpecker
in shining armour. Roo coo coo …
blood's in the shoe … to blindfold
freedom & not to shoot

What are we still waiting for?
For our meat to let us feel
its oestrogens

Shoot the votes off, shouts
the sea of the unemployed.

I am looking for the thread, the stitching:
words for wound dressing.

O yes, ambrosia
(Agamemnon, away on a job, who only knows
his son Orestes from photos)
before the milk starts to curdle!
Circe with smiling breasts:
If I could believe in the good
e.g. in men with biting calves
for stoppage-time afterplay, the 120th minute.

Pensioners at a tilt:
on their way home from the endgame where
the bar grew hard on the match. Stale

smell of the hard-to-place jobless.

Green Way is the name of the vinegar cleaners.

And yet:
Happiness in fat balls
come April, grey & velvet.

(for Gerhard Falkner)

Gerald Fiebig

ULRIKE DRAESNER
hiding

as a *haughty horse* (foreign tongue) swaying
and stiff regrettably not in the taxi but already
moved into my house my husband undressed other
women. the room scabbed up with fibrous walls so
you couldn't walk would have to fly the others
(fleeing) had him fused to their phones when
in the dark of this all-out scrabbling i became
the prince who could not stand the sight wrapped
in a fuck-flecked pony's coat. i'll show you
said my husband the variety of your own
inward traps you hyper-really are the wall
the chair the snake and yet-yet again the snow
flake the whitish bit of girlish grime trailing
its big own swollen eyes across the shaggy
deep-pile. really? trying to hammer it in?
made me think of that mole game where you had
to bash down black hills, with the other person
controlling the computer. fighting about a blind
thing forced back into its hole and practically
suffocating while still rowing tenderly
it strove to crawl right round the earth

Iain Galbraith

DİNÇER GÜÇYETER
The Mini Monks

Yılmaaaaaz! take the child to the barber, will you? tomorrow is Sugar Feast
this is how our Cleopatra kept the house in line
and quick as that, Papa and I were sitting with other fathers&sons
at the barber shop tucked between the mountains of Anatolia
I want a Jackie Chan cut I tell the uncle barber
a finger-long ash hangs from his cigarette
you got it, coming right up, he wheezes
grabs his hand-powered clippers and zips
back and forth across my scalp for a few minutes
that's not what Jackie Chan looks like
a mighty river flows down my cheeks
son, real men don't cry. this here is a 1989 cut
Jackie is an old-fashioned German dog
Papa consoles me with a coke
talks about heaven and earth for half an hour with the other papas
together they pull the world out of the mud, get up
and bring their mini monks back to the mothers

Caroline Wilcox Reul

NADJA KÜCHENMEISTER
at the base

no one quite knew how late it was
when it was too late: i came back
a breeze took my hand, the courtyard

recognized me, as always, without waking
i picked out the old names on the name plates
bein, puhahn, henke, brumm, i let them dry

no clothespins on the clothesline
where there was a puddle, no longer a puddle
where no trees stood, there stood trees

the hedge conversed with me, softly, a shadow
under the ping pong table, only the lifespan of the streetlights
seemed longer than an afternoon: mr. schatta

has slept in the graveyard for twenty-five years
for twenty-five years i have been asleep too
no one quite knows how late it is, when it is too late

benches without backrests, as always deli-counter light
the small flakes on my lips, that scrap of skin
i push around at the base of my tongue, i am.

Aimee Chor

YEVGENIY BREYGER
from **fugitive moons**

what happens when stones want to melt?
where do they fetch their melting material?
who brings them the inevitable tools?
what are viable chemical processes?

    when stones want to melt, they loot
    nuclear power plants, steal gigantic presses,
    uranium barrels. then they jump at each other.
    burst on the conveyor belt, begin to grow.

    asphalt splits streets, separates lovers
    from one another. school buildings relegate
    their teachers to flickering sports fields.
    fat children doze off on meadows.

how do ex-couples proceed without proximity?
how do schools distinguish teachers from
students? where can one be? how is one
not alone afterwards? and how alone?

Alexander Kappe

CHRISTIAN FILIPS
a white shoelace-

Flash now. This is
Momma's hand, how she knots! –

How to knot she teaches me
wants to teach him: she
sits in front of her son
ties the laces,
        so, both hands
hands both anticlockwise in the loop
does she
      – which way? this way? bunny ears-style

even herself know how, no, this way!
        not any further –

oh, mirror-inverted,
        Mother of God!
Soon we tie him
Soon he ties us

Jayashree Hari Joshi

PETER WATERHOUSE
In Praise of a Room

Wooden floor, white walls, the table and
two chairs (not foldable): such clarity
I have rarely seen elsewhere. All who enter here
say: good morning clarity. In the words of entering
foreigners: *good day you white walls.** Those
who say as much are enjoying the remoteness
from their own country (the question of such countries
has rarely arisen in this room). The lauding occupant
opens the window, closes the door. Anyone
would want to be a room like this. With regard
to the room the stranger thinks: *I could enter myself.* Thus
answering the ancient question. What question? The question
of the exceptions to be borne in mind. The question
of borders: where are ours? Is there
clarity before the border? Please open your
windows and take a seat on the chairs. Now
for the view outside. One says: the mill wheels are turning
(o, right, mill wheels), the flowers are embrangled
in their blooming, cats shut their eyes at night (behind closed eyes
the inner cat scorns all analogy, obviously). These events
occur for reasons of identity, as do our comparisons. Thus
our surroundings are fairly empty. Some still cry out:
here is a point (Archimedean, focal etc.). What follows of course
is pointing to the world. That (: reaching the object in question)
is too far for us all. So is our place
on this side? Yes. Where? A question for the foreigner:
what did you see on your various ways here? *Sorry
I don't understand.* Pardon me? now follows as the logical response
of someone without the language. The translator says: *turning wheels
occupation of flowers, the closing of the eye
of the cat.* Query: *which eye?* Answer:
both. Has nobody observed that
foreigners nod a lot? The visitor from abroad interrupts

all domestic philosophizing with the question: *may I have
a cup of tea?* It is good
that we are sitting in this room. I have seen
such clarity nirgendwo. Any occupant might choose
such a word (translatable as: *nowhere*). Query: can
we believe him? (Who is the occupant anyway, where
the room?) Supposing we have been
tricked, dodgily informed, lied to: who is the trickster? O
you trickster. If clarity were to obtain now
I would shout: let's scram. Or:
let's scram to a different room or a different different. Thus
the occupant of his own body speaks. Keiner hilft.
A translation for visitors from abroad: *Nobody
helps*.

* *English passages in the German poem are highlighted in italics.*

Iain Galbraith

SEBASTIAN UNGER
Ecstasy for Outsiders

This organic withholding in all approaching sentences
for antlers or worse, the sentence muscle

Hollow back in all activities, exclusion of liability
for glue and glass, finally tearing oneself off like a plaster

This upright gait in the stairs, chopped tree
the knotted hand in wood but as if without death

Being both, short and sweet when peeling potatoes
cutting through peel and skin, belonging

This intervention in the conversation of stone floor slabs
by a ringtone in front of an empty flat

Breaking into pieces but without interference, I mean
out of the plant silence of parsley gone mad

This restraining of everything without knowing it
lying awake in bed, on that side which is stronger

Being both, short and sweet when unlocking
rattling the keys, being on your last legs

Alexander Kappe

DİNÇER GÜÇYETER
The Green Cardigan

in this garden on a February evening / after the sleeping white colt was discovered buried under flakes / butterflies danced to the bağlama / in this garden / the coffin lay open on the divan of the dervishes / across it the green cloth / flung from the prayers of a woman / who had nothing more to say to this world / the final word I heard from her, *neither a funeral nor a wedding should ever be put off in this life* / that is the greatest sin / at the time I was the same age as the swing under the drainpipe

do you know how majestic the written hand can be? / in this garden / at its entrance / the yellowed letter still hangs between door and frame
Dearest Papa,
I've been in Germany for two months now, I'm doing well, though
sometimes I long for tarhana soup and fresh cheese. I found work
in a factory, will earn good money and who knows, maybe I
can buy myself a Mercedes someday. I'm enclosing 100 marks in
the envelope. When you go into town again, could you buy mother five meters of silk
with it. She should have a dress made and wear
it though the village, proud as a peacock. I still live with others
from the factory, when I get my own place, I'll send you the immigration paperwork
so you can apply for a visa. In quiet yearning I embrace
you both,
Yılmaz, Cologne, 1966
do you know / sometimes the years undertake their journey faster than the mail
in this garden / on the bare branches of the magnolia a skein of ants weaves each departure from silken thread / and the silenced crows / perched on the bicycle / do you know / how many languages they speak / this silence weighs more than all languages in the world / and don't you ask / whether a language can weigh anything / I saw / how a syllable became a roller, how it shaped the earth to linen / don't forget / behind every linen cloth a burned tongue cools

in this garden a little boy plays with his ball / a stage hangs at a tear in his jeans / where DJ Ronaldo spins records by Prince / yesterday the boy was sent to another team by his coach / he needs to learn to follow the rules / they might let him back later / the boy shoots the ball over the fence and bellows *goooooal* / that evening at bedtime he says to me:
Papa, who knows, maybe someday I'll be a pro footballer / I might get sooooo

rich, I can buy me a convertible, then I'll drive you to Aldi, promise! and don't laugh, Papa, you know, only the best players are allowed on my team
I hope, son, the years don't pass faster than your dreams / and now / close your sleepy eyes and drift off / we have a big day tomorrow / I will show you the dragon of the sea

and there behind that window, a man sits at his desk, maims words with his memories / gazes out the window / sees in the garden the divan of the boys / on their navels the copper weights of language / on a rusted cage under snowflakes he sees the green cardigan / and thinks / how many invisible knots this poem must have

Caroline Wilcox Reul

YEVGENIY BREYGER
from **fugitive moons**

careful,
do you not see this eagle?
it fixates on your youth.
discovers a dangerous subtext in its methods.
once you get used to it, it stops.
rather fixates on a box that you like.
containing two goat eyes. penetrate the box from the inside
with their goaty glee.
gently the wings of the eagle pat the earth,
even more gently
its claws separate aging from the process of aging.
yes, you both fear the winds,
but the true fear lies in the misdeed of distrust.
walk towards each other.
let this be your destiny.
or a dictate of early vice?
                you sat in a tram. not sure if as driver or wheel.
                to duck away
                from the content of the progressive environment.
                this experience was not objectifiable.
                the environment knew you in winter, already in winter
                it had forgotten you.
                the dream became firewood. you lay there,
                plagued by wood that inhabited you.
                o! your multiple body
                spread out on some old meadow, like a deposit.
                thirty days
                you lay there, a slimmed down tariff, without shelf life.
                and now?
i know you. i, myself, am the eagle.
i lay claim to this box.
i have also lain awake in the bushes,
don't look at me like that.
i am the messenger of foolishness, you are

its secret glow in the daytime,
no less delicate. please,
don't look at me like that. i want
to be a lazy watchdog and let you go.
you go, you go, you are gone.
now i stand there lonely, amid all the beautiful rubber.
now i fly away.
a wind blows around the imprint of a box.
the meadow carries its wood in the grass.

Alexander Kappe

BIRGIT KREIPE
this is my claim

this is my claim.
my carpenters have staked it out.

the way leading here is magic
i ran and i ran and found myself still in the same place

and the flakes, diminutive wind-whippets,
were chasing me, there was no short cut

just secret sequences of 90 steps
that no-one can memorise.

if i called – my voice came back alone
shut the window, will you, there's a draught.

the thirteen sad men in your eyes are freezing.
they're beckoning like chinese good-luck cats.

flakes are lying motionless outside the aviary.
the colours and tones around you, their amplitude fine

a thing that got lost in the wind.
every nine years, so it's said

you show yourself.
are you real? can i see you?

Catherine Hales

MONIKA RINCK
my gutless gob, muted by misery

THAT left me gobsmacked where, as someone else, i'd press
on without batting an eyelid, unperturbed, except it'd have to be
in a wardrobe, where i'd not be alone but in among priests.
there, between tracksuit trousers, terry bathrobes, negligees,
i could say it all, it'd flow from me freshly, as if i'd been manured.
finally, the burgeoning gaze of the priests would light on me
like the lavender sachet being tossed in, i'd curtsey at the sharp
crease of ironed laundry, i'd tidy the nylons away into the sock
drawer we once jokingly dubbed "hell's gullet". in the passage
of unfamiliar winter clothes, bering strait, priests would approach
me and, it being summer, would loosen my straps, quiet as dragonflies,
and teach me fear as something new which henceforth is somehow
part of the deal, to the applause of the discarded too-tight sweaters.
in another wardrobe at the same hour: a tennis tournament to mark
my big gob's reopening, with inaugural speeches and articled clerks.

Nicholas Grindell

POEM

ULJANA WOLF
little star-nosed mole speech

it's digging-dark in this poem, in which tongue could it possibly roam? turn on that star nose, fumble, rummage. here a small surface, silken folds. could be diced tofu. or toffee, if the edges were more rugged. everything rests with the edges, but where do i rest? *lingering, not even among what's most intimate.* long corridors, mixing of layers, well-aired, in short: terrine. or terrier snack. if only i could get away, outside, where the flags of tags wave, i'd find a word for my pretty pickle. *ah, where shall I find,* on these dark shelves of such clean speaking, where the mead, and where the me? i can hear coughing, a muffled trot, does he come nigh, the dog lover? bobby-mouth? the great trekker, yes: you go ahead and try to sell that, *lecker.*

Products that are sold in Germany must also be labeled in German.
—Erika Steinbach, member of the "Verein Deutsche Sprache"

Sophie Seita

ELKE ERB
Deliberation

Imagine to myself what I see are appearances.

And the appearances just apparent.

And the surface smooth.

But the appearance "dubious"
wouldn't be smooth like the others' wholeness,

instead wizened, a wizened hidden hole
in the others' wholeness.

As if something simmers, without boiling,
simmers coldly – dubious.

Bubbles.
That spot would hide the abyss.

And if a thought process
were adequately describable like this,

and described like this –
it would find itself defamed.

Amy Visram & Jana Maria Weiß

CHRISTIAN FILIPS
Begging Sentence for Clarity

where clarity lies open, so antagonistically open
and caught in the act: to understand the clarity
of the concept of clarity, like, let's say, if
there was a broad field, like if we said if
it was covered in snow, like if clear was also
from great distance: that's where my gaze lies
and it is and gazes so friendly foreign there
on the outward-stretching white lurking.

Shane Anderson

GEORG LESS
who is taking notes

wasn't that you, scary idea
in the rainy season on Lake Geneva? describing a way out with little arms
which leave the little legs unimpressed
knee-deep in action-packed prehistory, the putto wars
can be roughly divided into these five epochs: against
the void, against the stone, against the oil in which it drifts
against the enemy, against the scar that remains of the enemy
roughly repeats itself, if putto eats person
person becomes putto, biochemistry, putto becomes person, hunting sorcery
what does it eat, the person?

whilom put to flight by boredom, we are being kept on our toes
by the last mysteries of nutrition; that it tastes increasingly
familiar, no longer resists
the last questions of syntax and living space, we have to get twisty or get lost
I shouldn't leave the house without a desk at all, you say, write it down:
the removal men reach for the stars, in golden house dust
I shouldn't leave the house at all, get to know it in full detail, fill it up
did our goal no longer seem to be a win, but giving things a purely
      decorative spin?

Alexander Kappe

JAN KUHLBRODT
Shelf 1

Until recently, I thought I could work through the piles of books that had accumulated like files in an intelligence centre. Over time, however, they became a wall. Wall in front of the wall. They merged into an object that made further insulating material unnecessary.

Even when all the books were still on the shelves, they had long been organised haphazardly, and instead were arranged by size, since the formats larger than A4 were larger than quarto volumes and could only fit on the top and bottom shelves.

Now they lie in piles, stacked by size in rows, using the smallest space possible. We'll see; I'll wait for the utility bill. Of course, I hope that the arrangement of the spines will have an effect, a meaning. Insulation against a world that knows weather. Changes.

At the same time, I think the books also return something to me that could itself be a world. The world in microcosm? No, this expression only diminishes the thought. Not a small world! A paper world in which proportions play no role. An imaginary space. In it, notes pile up to form observations. Meticulous protocols. Descriptions of processes. Buildings. Reports.

And I now perceive them as a more or less disorganised pile of paper. Paper that once seemed organised, at least for a moment.

Field guides scattered in amongst them. Birdsong. Colours. Native reptiles. As a reminder of a reality that knows more than paper. Native fish.

A darkened specimen: Fauna in the Black Forest. A gift from my grandmother. She had brought it back from a trip to the West when I was perhaps ten and didn't really know what to do with it. But this book stayed with me for years, had not been weeded out or lost in one of the moves. And although it was now over forty years old, it seemed untouched.

At least I had started arranging the books after the shelf was put up, first by year of publication, then by subject. This way, I thought, I would be able to trace a course. A course of history whose order kept dissolving, at least here in the order of the books, as if physics wanted to prove its truth to me.

Entropy. The relentless increase in disorder along a timeline that was supposed to make order possible and disappears at its end, erasing the beginning. At any rate, this is how physicists claim we should imagine the Big Bang. Straightening events out into a sequence. Causality.

Yet the books turn more and more into a mountain of rubble which is piling up as history does in front of Benjamin's backward-flying angel. Perhaps order only exists outside of time. But not in an increasingly disorganised world. Order and comfort, and if not comfort, then a certain relief.

Yesterday I received news of the final collapse of Iraq, photographed by Chinese space travellers. The collapse was merely a claim. The photo showed the geography of Iraq, but not a vanishing political system.

I can imagine having been at the bottom of the photos myself, as a tiny shade of colour. Although I have never been to Iraq.

It's a pity that this event doesn't show up in the atlases as if by itself. The political order of the world, actualising itself in pictures. But then history would disappear from the shelf and I would have nothing to tell, nothing to remember.

*

It's been a long time since newspapers stopped coming into the house, and the ones that are already there are crumbling at the edges or are yellowed remnants from the times when I could afford a subscription, and from the times afterwards when I happily took advantage of free trial subscriptions if they were being offered somewhere, which automatically ended after a certain period of time, usually four weeks. Even today, employees from the marketing departments still call from time to time to see if I am interested in a subscription. I'm not.

I now get my information exclusively from the Internet. And from the radio. Fleeting events. Fleeting information. Topicality that is past as soon as you utter the word, topicality that eludes the present, doesn't wait until paper curls and turns yellow.

Otherwise, the paper wall around me would be even thicker and at some point all contact with the outside world would be lost. Newspapers are less about being up to date, they are storage. Storage devices for heat, you can burn them.

*

But if a pile of newspapers and journals were to fall over, I suddenly think, you could redistribute current events in a completely different context. Maybe that is what I do with the memories I have stored, stored like secret service reports, full of memories of events that I have experienced, survived, and of reports of events that I receive.

Alexander Kappe

ULRIKE DRAESNER
from HOW TO DO TE T(H)INKERING

sleep clash
    (philosopher in bed)

they say it's always (only)
a stalking of images
(finagling) of the horsetail
the arum spadix its fleshly-
cheeked imprint in the pillow
next morning
    anyone thinking "silky"?
think: "on paper"?
    they say it's ever
(never) a grasping
for the brain's looping
in pictures "thought(-)
    searches"
she never finds (-)herself
capable of composing a text
in a dream all its layers
(lurches) in tumbling ascent
    (inclined intent)
this fell-fool-
    translation into words
of the pillow's ear-lent lawn
    "sleep shelter sleep!"

while in the little theatre
in the evening the physicist
claimed: if she wanted to end
a dream she had (only)
to hurry to a tree
(consorting tree)
climb it
    and throw herself off
        to wake up in a world

of letters that fell in line yet
were utterly useless
    bluster bunk bludgeon
    of sleep

sleep mesh
    (physicist in bed)

(sleep's) inspiration
that recumbent instinct
that travels the inner life
of formulae the vastness
of blossoms cloud
and sheep
    on the pasture

against terror
    or horror of numbers
stapling of the self by
thoughts she
being the soul's dreams'
mesh. the sheep
    of sleep the curls
of its wool (vulgo: synaptic field)
        as a sprawling
turning and ever
turnable coherence
    (co-, here, love of all thought)
whereby infinity
that interval of real
numbers between zero and
    one would throw her
– crawling –
        – sucking –
    into the mossy

    base: the bed's cortex
    drowsy-cosy

    the philosopher meanwhile
    clubbing wants to push
    herself into every
    fold in matter
                 percussion party pistol
                 of sound

blindness of the thought's growth
    (philosopher taking a shower)

squidge-din
unthoughtlike still though not
simply visual either
the think-
    the mink-
        garret-ferrets up
glistening between synapses
a little sodium and life
psalmo- salmonskin (whose
metamorphoses too
upstream) scale of the dr… of
the drawatch drainage
    of the freshly hatched
still childly "at last come
into being we"

    that on our heads
we may carry second heads
that they might slip forth
            around
            us
marten-heads fishheads

our inventive caul: *19th c. infinity*
depiction of

Iain Galbraith

ANN COTTEN
Measured Gaze

My love for u is incommensurable,
when u r dressed it seems commensurable,
unrequited: not incomprehensible, in subtle
organization of a stanza, chiffon-chic: unwearable.

Supposed to be the same, yet falls out a or b,
hard to discern, without a rhyming clamp;
C seems familiar, no mistake, and d,
inverse, not quite it, makes one long for [blank].

Turn this way or turn that, transparently reverse,
depending how you come, you constantly rehearse
the passing-over of a crucial difference,
the error that will block your way from thence,
on non-replicability insisting,
maintaining that you know what you are missing.

Be it a couplet, be't tail rhyme, be't abba,
your adult life will bury all your social sins.
Go out now, sing along, and be the queens
of teenage innocence while knocking down the ladder

which, what with speed, we don't need anymore.
Wittgenstein says that since there is the cloud,
and since we say now what we dare to say out loud,
our selves no longer need to long to stretch before

us decades into speculation.
Instead, the mirror of our past grows dim,
we only see our dreams when we look in.
It's up to us to realize what we set our gaze on
by narratively reshaping the recent past below.

And yet, the more we gaze at it, it seems so vast.
Humours evaporate, blind days, iconoclast
nights in which ceiling fans chop up the dreams
that coat the tongue clapped round a one-eyed limb's
proud loathing of the moment. Prowling, frothing at the iambs'

cusps, fretting off in microfuturistic metres
forever now forlorn, and threadbare, too.
Much consciousness, self-conscious, teeters on
the brink of sleep. You're absent and yet there now, new,

uncertain what to want, the truth, though dismal, or the cunt
to mellow, welling untrue hope in which to wallow
for moments building up their realistic prowess. Hurt
a little bit, you find the edge that's always pending, fallow.

You never want to build, and now you hold the string,
uncut, unweighted. Wind it back into tight balls:
a technique kind of neat, although to make it sing
the kite must fly and pull it loose again. So, waiting for the wind,
you stand still as it banters, blows along the walls.
You don't know what it wants, but see your kite ascend.

(riffing on 'Lass deinen Drachen steigen' a Puhdys song
from the film *The Legend of Paul & Paula*)

Ann Cotten

ELKE ERB
Traversability

A succession of syllables, plus an emphasis:
Don't paths also move like language in time?

Deliberation down by the house, next to the pine.
It's hard to get away from here
from the lakeside, out of the mountains.

From above, from the third storey, the view into the tree:
Like a frond over the other of perpetual
                                             language
seems to paint something. Confined to this to and fro.

Location: Cadenabbia, Villa Collina, Lake Como
(upper house).

Amy Visram & Jana Maria Weiß

ULRIKE DRAESNER
what is poetry?

cleaning vacuuming wiping snot a scraped knee
tummy-stroking at bedtime or when it's sore singing
lullabies reading stories spreading your legs receptive
and soothing stuff dirty washing in drum fishing
pubic hair out of plughole for umpteenth time closing
toilet lid loading family's entire collection of mugs
left on top oft he dishwasher into machine cursing
but inaudibly pondering the upbringing of men
abandoning all upbringing bending to feed dog
playing parcheesi like a numpty at long last locking
oneself in the bathroom but one minute later total
pandemonium: wiping snot spreading jam sandwich
picking jam sandwich out of shag-pile washing
their swimsuits having not set a foot out all day
hunting the house-key admiring then despising
multi-tasking misheard as mummi-tasking shovel
dead bird off window-ledge not finding it icky
carrying it out to the garden taking in the solar storm
butterflies the stuff they've left by the pond (itself
desperately in need of cleaning) dragonflies
for seconds in the reflection: yourself
        bleary, small
        a child flashing its
        white teeth, your teeth

it is your body
you have no better word
        for what you see – vital
        and detached
        from yourself
knowing more about you than you
can bear it says: my love
for you is deeper than a forest

it says: dark is the inside of the mouth
and all that thinks

Iain Galbraith

DAGMARA KRAUS
from *gloomerang*

you race along the furlong,
                      crookeder than a barong,
                                        you go away,
                      u-bend again,
      in sidelong zippersong
      as in crabwalk;
                  so long as my foot is long,
          you'll always
come again,
                              but you can't be
        snagged
                circling and circling, *so long*,
     till you come,
                            alone all along,
sprung from the oak-rungs,
                you fan out, fangs out,
                      from your flightpath
                            (carving headlong
down the valleyslope),
                you return
        to me.
                        your spin
     returns—
            (oblong) a craving to
begin—
        it descends
              when you miss a target;
                    that's when the gong
gets rung.
                  and were it pyongyang,
                    you'd come back,
                you'd come with yin-yang,
              dugong, and oolong-scent,
            surrounded by linsangs,

                              christened in kelp.
                were it canaan,
                              you'd come back,
                       you'd come diaphanous
                as pale touch-me-not,
                       escorted by ten
                              sandaled vandals,
                genghis khan's courtesans,
                       their private scandals
                bandaged in green cellophane.
                       perhaps you'd come
                              by toboggan
                to my slack-walled wigwam,
                       with baboon-elan
                and legerdemain,
                       as mezzo-hetman
                  with a toucan-right-hand-man
                —the astrakhan mane
                       would suit you well.
                              you'd come back
                like a mustang,
                       you'd come trotting,
                completely frank
                       without salute or stink,
                sturm und drang or harangue,
                       but with quite correct
                oberek-step,
                you'd come back
                       as bridle, from scamming
                and summits. gloomerang,
           welcome back.

Joshua Daniel Edwin

ULJANA WOLF
to the dogs of kreisau

oh the skein of raggle-taggle village dogs: trickly
tails, stubbly legs, tough teeth fletching at the fence

yours is the street, the dust on an asphalt hem
yours the resonant night in the dormant valley

every echo is yours, the shivering repercussion
of sound from the hills, hierarchic growling

and bellowing barking: at first herculean, then hu-
mongous. reverberations recall hens in the know:

whoever doesn't loudly drive his drivel gets mobbed
by the pack, in brushfire throats the place loses itself

so crying wolf you survey the cosmos of this depression
dominating every route, every stranger, and me:

yours is my scent trail, my brave steps
yours are my calves finally out of the village

Brian Currid

ULJANA WOLF
postscript to the kreisau dogs

who says that poems are like these dogs
surrounded by their own echo at the village core

of the waiting and pawing at half moon
of the stubborn marking of language terrains –

he knows you not, you frantic barkers
cassandras in wallachia's sonic reverie

you bring what's called and what's calf
in a foolhardy bite from behind

together as if a leg were but a leaf
and the order of things a trade:

in one of my boots still the imprint
of your teeth, a gnarly four nips

that's your reward for a pursuant verse
the world follows poetry at heel

Brian Currid

ELKE ERB
Suspicion of a Poem

Lying on the bed, face down, reading

(recovering)
(in spiritual discipline).

My lower back hurts a little.

As I become aware of it,

the arch of a bridge rises
high in front of me.

Why, I think, that now?

– I give my lower back some air …

Below us are grassy banks … water …

Suspicion of a poem.

– When I write poems. – perhaps also with other things, I am the source, nothing more – and how I love now that I'm writing it the spring water that I see emerging from between the rocks, and around them…!! the tiny divisions …, the dark ground, the light, the small, round mirrors, the little eddies…

14.12.16

Shane Anderson

About the authors and translators

Anderson, Shane (b. 1982). Translator of *The Great Nowitzki* by Thomas Pletzinger (2022), *A poem is what it does* by Elke Erb (2018), and *The Amme Talks* by Ulf Stolterfoht (2017). Author of *After the Oracle* (2021), *Soft Passer* (2015), and *Etudes* (2012).

Beals, Kurt (b. 1980). Translator of *All Quiet on the Western Front* by Erich Maria Remarque (2025), *Things That Disappear* by Jenny Erpenbeck (2025), *The Steppenwolf* by Hermann Hesse (2023), *engulf – enkindle* by Anja Utler (2010).

Breyger, Yevgeniy (b. 1989). Poet and translator. Publications include *Frieden ohne Krieg* (2023), *Gestohlene Luft* (2020), *flüchtige monde* (2016). Translations of his poetry into English have appeared in *No Man's Land*, *Notre Dame Review* and on *lyrikline.org*.[1]

Brocke, Sonja vom (b. 1980). Poet, essayist and academic. Publications include *Mush* (2020), *Düngerkind* (2018), *Venice singt* (2015). Translations of her poetry into English have appeared on *lyrikline.org*.

Bulucz, Alexandru (b. 1987). Poet and critic. Publications include *Stundenholz* (2024), *was Petersilie über die Seele weiß* (2020), *Aus sein auf uns* (2016). Translations of his poetry into English have appeared in *Versopolis* and on *lyrikline.org*.

Campbell, Paul-Henri (b. 1982). Translator of *Love After Love* by Ilma Rakusa (2021), *All Ears* by Ludwig Steinherr (2000/2013). Author of *innere organe* (2022), *nach den narkosen* (2017), *Am Ende der Zeilen* (2013).

Callies, Carolin (b. 1980). Poet and podcast host. Publications include *teilchenzoo* (2023), *schatullen & bredouillen* (2019), *fünf sinne & nur ein besteckkasten* (2015). Translations of her poetry into English have appeared in *No Man's Land*.

Chor, Aimee (b. 1972). Poet and translator. Translator of poems by Nadja Küchenmeister in *The Paris Review* 246 (2023), *Circumference Magazine* 12 (2024).

Cotten, Ann (b. 1982). Poet and translator. Author of *Lather in Heaven* (2016), *Die Anleitungen der Vorfahren* (2023), among others. Co-editor of *Triëdere*, Austrian journal for theoretical literature. Translator of *Alles was passiert* (2019) by Joe Wenderoth, *Geile Deko* (2019) and *Vielleicht ging es immer darum, dass wir Feuer spucken* (original: *STERLING KARAT GOLD*, 2024) by Isabel Waidner, *Glitch Feminismus* (2021) by Legacy Russell, *Krieg und Paradies* (2022) by Adam Green.

Currid, Brian (b. 1970). Translator and independent scholar. Poetry translations featured in collections online and in several journals. Author of several articles and the book *A National Acoustics: Music and Mass Publicity in Weimar and Nazi Germany* (2006).

---

[1] https://www.lyrikline.org/en/home/

Draesner, Ulrike (b. 1962). Poet, translator, novelist and academic. Publications include *Doggerland* (2021), *subsong* (2014), *berührte orte* (2008), *kugelblitz* (2005), *Gedächtnisschleifen* (1995). Translations of her poetry into English include *this porous fabric* (2022) trans. by Iain Galbraith. Translator into German of Louise Glück and Gertrude Stein.

Duncan, Andrew (b. 1956). Poet, translator, editor and critic. Translator of Thomas Kling, *zerodrifter: Selected Poems 1983–2005* (2019). His own work includes *With Feathers on Glass* (2023), *On the Margins of Great Empires: Selected Poems* (2018), *Threads of Iron* (2013), *In Five Eyes* (2013). His many critical works include *Beautiful Feelings of Sensitive People* (2024), *Nothing is being suppressed* (2022) and *The Failure of Conservatism in Modern British Poetry* (2nd edn., 2016). Editor of *Angel Exhaust* (1992–98; 2005–).

Edwin, Joshua Daniel (b. 1982). Translator of *gloomerang* by Dagmara Kraus (2014). Author of *Modern Audubon* (2019).

Egger, Oswald (b. 1963). Poet and visual artist. Publications include *Val di non* (2017), *Nichts, das ist* (2001), *Die Herde der Rede* (1999). Translations of his poetry into English include *Room of Rumor: Tunings* (2004) trans. by Michael Pisaro.

Erb, Elke (1938–2024). Poet, translator and critic. A selection of her poetry recently appeared as *Das ist hier der Fall. Ausgewählte Gedichte* (2020). Translations of her poetry into English include *A poem is what it does* (2018) trans. by Shane Anderson, and *Mountains in Berlin* (1995) trans. by Rosmarie Waldrop.

Falb, Daniel (b. 1977). Poet and theorist. Publications include *Deutschland. Ein Weltmärchen (in leichter Sprache)* (2023), *Orchidee und Technofossil* (2019), *CEK* (2015), *die räumung dieser parks* (2003). Translations of his poetry into English have appeared in *No Man's Land* and on *lyrikline.org*.

Fenwick, Christopher (b. 1986). Writer, translator and researcher. Author of *Literature and Ethics Beyond Skepticism* (2025)

Fiebig, Gerald (b. 1973). Author, translator, sound artist. Translator of *Wind Sleeping in a Silk Tree* by Tom Schulz (2025), *Player Time* by Simon Jenner (1998) and other translations published in various magazines. Author of *motörhead klopstöck* (2020), *nach dem nachkrieg* (2017).

Filips, Christian (b. 1981). Poet and director. A selection of his poetry recently appeared as *Im Traum die Auskunft sagt: Hier! Ausgewählte Gedichte 1996–2023* (2023). Translations of his poetry into English have appeared on *lyrikline.org*.

Galbraith, Iain (b. 1956). Translator of *this porous fabric* by Ulrike Draesner (2022), *The Unfinished* by Reinhard Jirgl (2020), *River* by Esther Kinsky (2018), *Self-portrait with a Swarm of Bees* by Jan Wagner (2015). Author of *The True Height of the Ear* (2018), *Aus dem kleinen Zimmer* (2024).

Gillett, Robert. Poet, translator, academic. Translator of *The Feather-Duster Song* by Anija Seedler and Sudabeh Mohafez (2019), *Umbrage* by Anija Seedler and Sudabeh Mohafez (2020) as well as translations in academic publications including Friederike Mayröcker (*Austrian Studies*, 2004), Richard Leising (*German Life and Letters*, 2014), Kerstin Hensel (*Kerstin Hensel: Literary Correspondences*, 2025). Academic work on translation includes *Queer in Translation* (edited, with B.J. Epstein, 2017).

Grindell, Nicholas (b. 1968). Translator of *to refrain from embracing* (2011) and *Honey Protocols* (2025), both by Monika Rinck. Author of *There was an Old Man of Berlin* (2022), *You keep having the same dream…* (2024).

Güçyeter, Dinçer (b. 1979). Poet and publisher. Publications include *Mein Prinz, ich bin das Ghetto* (2021), *Aus Glut geschnitzt* (2017), *Ein Glas Leben* (2012). Translations of his poetry into English include *ANMLY*, *Tupelo Quarterly* and on *lyrikline.org*.

Hales, Catherine (b. 1956). Translator of *Berlin Fresco* by Norbert Hummelt (2010), *totenmaske/death mask* by Anna Hoffmann (2010), *Babylon Transit* by Anna Hoffmann (2024) and in various magazines. Author of *hazard or fall* (2010), *feasible stratagems* (2013).

Hawkey, Christian (b. 1969). Translator of *Bad words: selected short prose* by Ilse Aichinger (2018, with Uljana Wolf). Author of *Sift* (2021), *Sonne from Ort* (2012, with Uljana Wolf), *Ventrakl* (2010), *Citizen of* (2007), *The Book of Funnels* (2004).

Hefter, Martina (b. 1965). Poet and performance artist. Publications include *In die Wälder gehen, Holz für ein Bett klauen* (2020), *Es könnte auch schön werden* (2018), *Ungeheuer. Stücke/Gedichte* (2016), *Nach den Diskotheken* (2010). Translations of her poetry into English have appeared on *lyrikline.org*.

Igel, Jayne-Ann (b. 1954). Poet. Publications include *wolken hinterm rollo* (2024), *wir ländern uns fort* (2022), *Vor dem Licht / Umtriebe* (2014) *Unerlaubte Entfernung* (2004), *Bernd Igel* (1989).

Jackson, Hendrik (b. 1971). Poet, essayist and translator. Publications include *Panikraum* (2018), *Im Licht der Prophezeiungen* (2012), *Im Innern der zerbrechenden Schale* (2007), *Dunkelströme* (2006), *Einflüsterungen von seitlich* (2001). Translations of his poetry into English have appeared in *No Man's Land*, *Versopolis* and on *lyrikline.org*.

Joshi, Jayashree Hari (b. 1966). Poet, translator and essayist. Translated and published several German and English plays, novels, articles, essays, children's literature and poetry.

Kappe, Alexander (b. 1987). Translator of *the locality principle* by Keith Waldrop (2023), *The Real Subject: Queries and Conjectures of Jacob Delafon; With Sample Poems* by Keith Waldrop (2025). Author of *nachreden auf dunkelengel* (2023).

Kling, Thomas (1957–2005). Poet. His collected poems appeared as *Gesammelte Gedichte* (2006); his collected works appeared in four volumes as *Werke* (2020). Translations of his poems into English include *zerodrifter: Selected Poems 1983–2005* (2019) trans. Andrew Duncan.

Kraus, Dagmara (b. 1981). Poet and translator. Publications include *liedvoll, deutschyzno* (2020), *das vogelmot schlich mit geknickter schnute* (2015), *kummerang* (2012). Selected translations into English: *gloomerang* (2014) trans. by Joshua Daniel Edwin.

Kreipe, Birgit (b. 1964). Poet. Publications include *Aire* (2021), *SOMA* (2016), *wenn ich wind sage seid ihr weg* (2010). Translations of her poetry into English have appeared in *No Man's Land* and on *lyrikline.org*.

Küchenmeister, Nadja (b. 1981). Poet. Publications include *Im Glasberg* (2020), *Unter dem Wacholder* (2014), *Nachbild* (2009). Translations of her poetry into English have appeared in *VOLUME, Paris Review, No Man's Land, Apple Valley Review, Mayday Magazine* and on *lyrikline.org*.

Kuhlbrodt, Jan (b. 1966). Poet, essayist and dramatist. Publications include *Die Rückkehr der Tiere* (2020), *Stötzers Lied. Gesang vom Leben danach* (2013), *Verzeichnis* (2006).

Leeder, Karen (b. 1962). Author, translator, literary scholar. Translator of *Shining Sheep* by Ulrike Almut Sandig (2023), *Psyche Running: Selected Poems 2005–2022* by Durs Grünbein (2024), *In a Cabin, in the Woods* by Michael Krüger (2024) and in various magazines.

Leß, Georg (b. 1981). Poet and essayist. Publications include *die Nacht der Hungerputten* (2023), *die Hohlandmusikalität* (2019), *Schlachtgewicht* (2013). Translations of his poetry into English have appeared on *lyrikline.org*.

Mayröcker, Friederike (1924–2021). Poet. A selection of her poetry was published as *Gesammelte Gedichte 1939–2003* (2005). Translations of her poetry into English include *études* (2023) trans. by Donna Stonecipher, *Communicating Vessels. Two Portraits of Grief* (2021) trans. by Alexander Booth, and *Raving Language: Selected Poems 1946–2005* (2007) trans. by Richard Dove.

Meckel, Christoph (1935–2020). Poet and graphic novelist. A selection of his poetry appeared as *Tarnkappe. Gesammelte Gedichte* (2015). Translations of his poetry into English have appeared in *Circumference* and other magazines.

Nissan, Grace (b. 1992). Poet, translator. Selected works as translator: *kochanie today i bought bread* by Uljana Wolf (2023), *War Diary* by Yevgenia Belorusets (2023). Selected works as author: *The Utopians* (2025), *The City Is Lush With / Obstructed Views* (2019).

Popp, Steffen (b. 1978). Poet, translator and academic. Publications include *118* (2017), *Kolonie Zur Sonne* (2008), *Wie Alpen* (2004). Translations of his poetry into English have appeared on *lyrikline.org*. Translator into English of Elizabeth Bishop and Ben Lerner.

Preiwuß, Kerstin (b. 1980). Poet, novelist and essayist. Publications include *Heute ist mitten in der Nacht* (2023), *Gespür für Licht* (2016), *Nachricht von neuen Sternen* (2006). Translations of her poetry into English have appeared in *No Man's Land* and *lyrikline.org*.

Reul, Caroline Wilcox (b. 1965). Translator of *In the morning we are glass* by Andra Schwarz (2021), *Who lives* by Elisabeth Borchers (2017).

Rinck, Monika (b. 1969). Poet, essayist and academic. Publications include *Alle Türen* (2019), *zum fernbleiben der umarmung* (2007), *Verzückte Distanzen* (2004). Translations of her poetry into English include *to refrain from embracing* (2011) and *Honey Protocols* (2025), both trans. by Nicholas Grindell.

Sandig, Ulrike Almut (b. 1979). Poet, novelist and performance artist. Publications include *Leuchtende Schafe* (2022), *ich bin ein Feld voller Raps, verstecke die Rehe und leuchte wie dreizehn Ölgemälde übereinandergelegt* (2016), *Zunder* (2005). Translations of her work into English include *Shining Sheep* (2023), *Monsters like us* (2022), *I am a field full of rapeseed, give cover to deer and shine like thirteen oil paintings laid one on top of the other* (2020), *Thick of it* (2018), *Grimm* (2018), all trans. by Karen Leeder.

Schmidt, Bradley (b. 1979). Translator and lecturer. Translator of *Missing Witness* by Ulrike Almut Sandig (2015). Numerous individual translations published online and in print journals.

Schneider, Jake (b. 1988). Yiddish cultural activist. Translator of *Fragmented Waters* by Ron Winkler (2016), *Underground Modernity* by Alfrun Kliems (2021). His Yiddish poems have appeared in *Afn Shvel, Yiddish Branzhe, Yiddishland*.

Scho, Sabine (b. 1970). Poet and photographer. Publications include *Haus für einen Boxer* (2021), *Tiere in Architektur* (2013), *farben* (2008), *Album* (2001). Translations of her work into English have appeared in *The Origin of Values O – Pantanal* (2021) and *The Origin of Senses: an Intervention* (2015, trans. by Ann Cotten).

Schulz, Tom (b. 1970). Poet and critic. Publications include: *Briefe aus der Roten Wüste* (with Maria Borio, 2024), *Die Erde hebt uns auf* (2024), *Reisewarnung für Länder Meere Eisberge* (2019). Translations of his poetry into English include *Wind Sleeping in a Silk Tree* (2025), trans. by Gerald Fiebig.

Scott, Joel (b. 1983). Poet and translator. Translator of *The Aesthetics of Resistance*, volumes 2 and 3 (2020 and 2025) by Peter Weiss. Author of the chapbooks *Bildverbot* (2017) and *Diary Farm* (2014).

Seel, Daniela (b. 1974). Poet and publisher. Publications include *Nach Eden* (2024), *was weißt du schon von prärie* (2015), *ich kann diese stelle nicht wiederfinden* (2011). Translations of her poetry into English have appeared in *Versopolis* and on *lyrikline.org*.

Seita, Sophie. Artist, researcher, translator. Translator of *Subsisters: Selected Poems* (2017) and *i mean i dislike that fate that i was made to where* (2015), both by Uljana Wolf. Author of *Fantasias in Counting* (2014), *My Little Enlightenment Plays* (2020), *Lessons of Decal* (2023).

Stauffer, Verena (b. 1978). Poet. Publications include *Kiki Beach* (2025), *Ousia* (2020), *Orchis* (2018). Translations of her poetry into English have appeared in *No Man's Land* and on *lyrikline.org*.

Stolterfoht, Ulf (b. 1963). Poet, essayist and translator. Publications include *neu-jerusalem* (2015), *wider die wiesel* (2013), *holzrauch über heslach* (2007), *fach-*

sprachen I–IX (2005). Translations of his poetry into English include *The Amme Talks* (2017) by Shane Anderson, and *Lingos I–IX* (2007), trans. by Rosmarie Waldrop. Translator into German of J.H. Prynne and Gertrude Stein.

Stonecipher, Donna. Poet and translator. Translator of *études* (2020) and *cahier* (2024) by Friederike Mayröcker. Author of *The Ruins of Nostalgia* (2023), *Transaction Histories* (2018) and *Model City* (2015).

Thießen, Lotta (b. 1988). Translator of *This Energy Wasted by Flight* (Pamenar Press, 2023) by Lotte L.S. and *Hardly War* by Don Mee Choi (forthcoming with Spector Books 2025). Author of *Coineaters in Progress* (Cutt Press 2024) and *Fragments of Baby* (Materialien 2019).

Thomas, Nicola (b. 1987). Translator, poet and academic. Author of *Space, Place and Poetry in English and German 1960–1975* (2018) and essays. Her poems have appeared in various magazines.

Unger, Sebastian (b. 1978). Poet and essayist. Publications include *Das Pferd als sein eigener Reiter* (2024), *Die Tiere wissen noch nicht Bescheid* (2018). Translations of his poetry into English have appeared on *lyrikline.org*.

Utler, Anja (b. 1973). Poet, essayist and translator. Publications include *Es beginnt. Trauerrefrain* (2023), *jana, vermacht* (2009) *brinnen* (2006), *münden – entzüngeln* (2004). Translations of her poetry into English include the forthcoming *So the day begins*, trans. by Kurt Beals and Aimee Chor, and *engulf – enkindle* (2010) trans. by Kurt Beals. Translator into German of Anne Carson.

Visram, Amy (b. 1982). Translator of numerous texts for titles published by specialist academic presses. Author of *My Four Seasons* (2017).

Waterhouse, Peter (b. 1956). Poet and translator. Publications include *von herbstlicher Stille umgeben wird ein Stück gespielt* (2003) *Prosperos Land* (2001), *Passim* (1986), *Menz* (1984). Translations of his work include *Language Death Night Outside*, a "poem/novel", trans. Rosmarie Waldrop (2009). Translator into English of Michael Hamburger.

Weiß, Jana Maria (b. 1992). Translator and researcher. Translator of poems by Edward Dorn, Alice Notley and Eugene Ostashevsky for *Neue Rundschau*, *Edit* and *Schreibheft*. Her literary essays have appeared in *Bildfäden* and *Transistor*.

Wolf, Uljana (b. 1979). Poet and translator. Publications include *Muttertask* (2023), *meine schönste lengevitch* (2013), *Sonne from Ort* (2012), *Falsche Freunde* (2009), *kochanie ich habe brot gekauft* (2005). Translations of her poetry into English include *kochanie, today i bought bread* (2023). *Subsisters: Selected Poems* (2017), *i mean i dislike that fate that i was made to where* (2015), and *False Friends* (2009), all trans. by Sophie Seita.

Acknowledgements

BREYGER, YEVGENIY, extracts from *frieden ohne krieg* (kookbooks, 2023); 'Königreich der verschluckten Muschel', 'Königreich des Regens' and 'Königreich des weiten Wegs' from *Gestohlene Luft* (kookbooks, 2020); and extracts from *flüchtige monde* (kookbooks, 2016), used by permission of the publisher. VOM BROCKE, SONJA, 'Kunde' and 'Echolots Zornesmahl' from *Venice singt* (kookbooks, 2015), used with permission of the publisher. 'Lore' and 'Sonar's supper of wrath', translated by Catherine Hales, first appeared on lyrikline.org, reprinted with permission of the translator. BULUCZ, ALEXANDRU, 'Zur Henkersmahlszeit mit der Erinnerungskutsche I', 'Sieben Dignitäten. Notre Dame de Paris et des Fleurs. 15. April 2019 ff., o' and 'Gespräche mit Baumrinden II' from *Was Petersilie über die Seele weiß* (Schöffling, 2020), used with permission of the publisher. 'Kreischqueller Heuweg' from *Stundenholz* (Schöffling, 2024), used with permission of the publisher. 'To the Last Meal by Memory Carriage I', 'Seven Dignitites. Notre Dame de Paris et des Fleurs. April 15, 2019 ff.' and 'Conversations with Tree Bark II' translated by Jake Schneider, first appeared on lyrikline.org, reprinted with permission of the translator. CALLIES, CAROLIN, 'ein schlachtfeld aus beinen' and 'das zwitschern ist ein kleines biest' from *schatullen & bredouillen* (Schöffling, 2019), used by permission of the publisher. COTTEN, ANN, 'Ellen Blick', 'Extension, Besitz' and 'Homologie, ich' taken from *Fremdwörterbuchsonette. Gedichte.* © Suhrkamp Verlag Frankfurt am Main 2007; 'ICE' and 'Größe, Prokrastination' from *Florida-Räume* © Suhrkamp Verlag Berlin 2010; and 'Ökoschotter' from *Die Anleitungen der Vorfahren* © Suhrkamp Verlag Berlin 2023. All rights reserved by and controlled through Suhrkamp Verlag Berlin. 'Measured Gaze', 'Extension, Possession' and 'Homology, Myself', translated by Ann Cotten, first appeared on lyrikline.org, reprinted by permission of the translator. DRAESNER, ULRIKE, extracts from 'HOW TO DO TE T(H)**INKERING**' (2021), first published by *Transistor* magazine, used with permission of the author. 'what is poetry?' and 'hiding' from *Subsong* (Luchterhand Verlag, 2014), used with permission of the publisher. 'what is poetry?' and 'hiding' translated by Iain Galbraith, first published in *this porous fabric* (Shearsman Books, 2022), reprinted with permission of the translator. EGGER, OSWALD, 'Sommern' from *Herde der Rede. Poem.* © Suhrkamp Verlag Frankfurt am Main 1999. All rights by and controlled through Suhrkamp Verlag Berlin. ERB, ELKE, 'Gedichtverdacht' from *Gedichtverdacht* (roughbooks, 2019); 'Passierbarkeit' and 'Erwägung' from *Gänsesommer* (2005); 'Nach meinem Ermessen' and 'Heidelberg, Hotel' from *Sonanz* (Urs Engeler, 2008), all used by permission of Akademie der Künste Berlin. FALB, DANIEL, extracts from *die räumung dieser parks* (kookbooks, 2003) and from *CEK* (kookbooks 2015), used by permission of the publisher. Extracts from *the clearance of these parks* translated by Brian Currid and from *CEK* translated by Christian Hawkey, first appeared on lyrikline.org, reprinted by permission of the translators.

FILIPS, CHRISTIAN 'ein weißer Schnürsenkel-' from *Der Scheiße-Engel. Eine Analyse* (2015). 'Heischesatz zur Klarheit' from *Heiße Fusionen Eins* (roughbooks, 2010). 'A white shoelace' translated by Jayashree Hari Joshi and 'Begging Sentence for Clarity' translated by Shane Anderson, first appeared on lyrikline.de, reprinted by permission of the translators. GÜÇYETER, DINÇER, 'die grüne Strickjacke', 'die Mini-Mönche' and extract from 'ein Brief, nach 35 Jahren', first published in *Mein Prinz, ich bin das Ghetto* (ELIF, 2021), used by permission of the publisher. HEFTER, MARTINA, extracts from *In die Wälder gehen, Holz für ein Bett klauen* (kookbooks, 2020) used with permission of the publisher. IGEL, JAYNE-ANN, 'Das blaue blut der flußläufe' first published in *Umtriebe* (gutleut, 2013); 'Grüne grenze' and 'Im status der unwägbarkeit' first published in *die stadt hielt ihre flüsse im verborgenen* (gutleut, 2019), reprinted with permission of the publisher. JACKSON, HENDRIK, 'freeze frame' and 'Selbstporträt mit Sülze' from *Dunkelströme* (kookbooks, 2006); 'schutz vor nachstellungen – meiner vorstellung nach' from *Im Licht der Prophezeiungen* (kookbooks, 2012), used by permission of the publisher. 'weather fields / freeze frame' translated by Catherine Hales, first appeared on lyrikline.org, reprinted by permission of the translator. KLING, THOMAS, 'ratinger hof, zb 1', 'ratinger hof, zb 2' taken from: Thomas Kling, *Werke in vier Bänden. Werke I. Gedichte 1977–1991*. Herausgegeben von Marcel Beyer in Zusammenarbeit mit Frieder von Ammon, Peer Trilcke und Gabriele Wix. © Suhrkamp Verlag Berlin 2020. 'larven' from *erprobung herzstärkender mittel / brennstabm / nacht. sicht. gerät. Ausgewählte Gedichte 1981– 1993* © Suhrkamp Verlag Frankfurt am Main 1994. All rights reserved by and controlled through Suhrkamp Verlag Berlin. 'serner, karlsbad' and 'falknerei' from *morsch. Gedichte* © Suhrkamp Verlag, Frankfurt am Main, 1996. All rights reserved by and controlled through Suhrkamp Verlag Berlin. 'ratinger hof, documentary report 1', 'ratinger hof, documentary report 2', 'ghosts', 'serner, karlsbad' and 'falconry' translated by Andrew Duncan, first published in *zerodrifter: Selected Poems* (Shearsman Books, 2019), reprinted by permission of the translator. KRAUS, DAGMARA, 'nur mut, mond' and other extracts from *kummerang* (kookbooks, 2012), used by permission of the publisher. 'be brave, moon' and other extracts from *kummerang*, translated by Joshua Daniel Edwin, first published in *gloomerang* (Argos, 2014), reprinted by permission of the translator. KREIPE, BIRGIT, 'hier ist mein claim', 'on two trees', from *SOMA* (kookbooks, 2016); 'december is a rhino' from aire (kookbooks, 2021); 'hexe k' and 'training beim weißen mann' from *schönheitsfarm* (Verlagshaus Berlin, 2012), used by permission of the publisher. KÜCHENMEISTER, NADJA, 'am grund', 'letzte signale', 'es beginnt, wo es endet' from *Im Glasberg* (Schöffling, 2020), used by permission of the publisher. 'it begins where it ends' first appeared in *mercury firs* 3, 2023; 'at the base' first appeared in *Four Way Review* 27, 2023. KUHLBRODT, JAN, 'Regal 1' and 'Im Haus gegenüber' from *Die Rückkehr der Tiere* (Verlagshaus Berlin 2020), used by permission of the publisher. LESS, GEORG, 'fünfter Wirbel / wir belagerten' from *die Hohlhandmusikalität* (kookbooks, 2019); 'eine

Putte oder eine Person' and 'wer mitschreibt' from *Die Nacht der Hungerputten* (kookbooks, 2023). 'fifth vertebra / we beleaguered' translated by Chris Fenwick, first appeared on lyrikline.org, reprinted by permission of the translator. MAYRÖCKER, FRIEDERIKE, 'tiefblauer mai, wallend' and 'tropisches Knabenkraut, wild, im Schnabel' taken from: Friederike Mayröcker, *Gesammelte Gedichte 1939–2003*. Herausgegeben von Marcel Beyer. © Suhrkamp Verlag Frankfurt am Main 2004; extract from *études* © Suhrkamp Verlag Berlin 2013. All rights reserved by and controlled through Suhrkamp Verlag Berlin. Extract from *études* (Seagull, 2019) translated by Donna Stonecipher, reprinted by permission of the publisher. MECKEL, CHRISTOPH, 'Bericht vom Kind', 'Aschegoldasche', 'Windrädchen' from *Für Clarisse* (gutleut, 2018), used with permission of the publisher. POPP, STEFFEN, 'Fenster zur Weltnacht', 'Tannen, das Grenzland' and 'Elegie für K.' from *Wie Alpen* (kookbooks, 2004); 'Fußnoten aus dem Antikenheft', 'Nach dem Gewehrfeuer II', 'Selbstporträt am Renaissancefenster' and 'Auratische Flurkunde' from *Kolonie Zur Sonne* (kookbooks, 2008); extract from *Dickicht mit Reden und Augen* (kookbooks, 2013), all used with permission of the publisher. 'Elegy for K.' translated by Donna Stonecipher and 'Auratic Agrology' translated by Christian Hawkey, first appeared on lyrikline.org, used with permission of the translators. PREIWUSS, KERSTIN, 'sieben' from *Rede. Gedichte*. © Suhrkamp Verlag Berlin 2012. All rights reserved by and controlled through Suhrkamp Verlag Berlin. RINCK, MONIKA, 'bitte wie geht vorbereiten', 'was ist mit den tieren?', 'das gegenteil von verführung', '*supercortemaggiore!*', 'orpheus charmiert bestien minderer qualität' and 'meine stumme fresse feige vor tristesse' from *zum fernbleiben der umarmung* (kookbooks, 2007); 'der letzte tag im süden' and 'trainingsziele' from *Verzückte Distanzen* Lyrik Edition. Neue Ausgabe, issued by Heinz Kattner (Springe: zu Klampen, 2013), p. 13 and p. 33, used by permission of the publisher. 'pray how does getting ready work?', 'what about the animals?', 'the opposite of seduction', '*supercortemaggiore!*', 'orpheus charms beasts of lesser quality', 'my gutless gob, muted by misery', translated by Nicholas Grindell, first published in *to refrain from embracing* (Burning Deck, 2011), reprinted with permission of the publisher. SANDIG, ULRIKE ALMUT, extract from 'Gesang des Funkturms' from *Leuchtende Schafe* (Schöffling, 2022), used with permission of the publisher. Extract from 'Songs of the Radio Tower' translated by Karen Leeder, first published in *Shining Sheep* (Seagull, 2023), used with permission of the publisher. SCHO, SABINE, 'skin' and 'die startklaren Maschinen' from *Farben* (kookbooks, 2008), used with permission of the publisher; extract from *The Origin of Values* (Villa Aurora Thomas Mann House, 2021); 'skin' first appeared on lyrikline.org, used with permission of the translator. SCHULZ, TOM, 'Das Leben wiederholt sich', 'Abends, im Lidl steht die Arbeiterklasse an' from *Abends im Lidl* (Krash/Stahl-Verlag 2004); 'Ringbahn' from *Vergeuden, den Tag* (kookbooks, 2006), used with permission of the author. All translations from *Wind Sleeping in a Silk Tree* (Waterloo Press 2025), used with permission of the translator and publisher. SEEL, DANIELA, 'SAGA' from *was weißt du schon von prärie* (kookbooks, 2015), used with permission of the author. STAUFFER, VERENA. 'Ling' Ling' from *Ousia* (kookbooks, 2020), used with permission of the publisher. Translation first appeared on lyrikline.de, used with permission of the translator. STOLTERFOHT, ULF, 'die fünfundvierzig blutjesus-legenden' from *neu-jerusalem* (kookbooks, 2015), used by permission of the publisher. UNGER, SEBASTIAN. 'Der ungebändigte Dompteur', 'Zeichenlehre (B. F. Electrics', 'Ausser sich', 'Borametz – Das pflanzliche Lamm' from *Die Tiere wissen noch nicht Bescheid* (Matthes & Seitz, 2018), used with permission of the publisher. 'Borametz' and 'The Untied Tamer' translated by Ann Cotten, first appeared on lyrikline.de, reprinted by permission of the translator. UTLER, ANJA. 'für daphne: geklagt' from *münden—entzüngeln* (Edition Korrespondenzen, 2004), used with permission of the publisher. 'for daphne: lamented' translated by Kurt Beals, first published in *engulf – enkindle* (Burning Deck, 2010), reprinted by permission of the translator. WATERHOUSE, PETER. 'Umgang mit Abständen', 'Lob eines Zimmers' from *MENZ* (Droschl, 1987); 'Im Garten sitzend ohne Entsprechung', 'Am Tag des engen Gedankens' and 'Zweifel an Straßenbahnen' from *passim* (Rohwolt, 1986), used with permission of the author. 'Doubts about Trams', translated by Iain Galbraith, first published in *New England Review*, Vol 37 Issue 3 (2016), reprinted by permission of the translator. WOLF, ULJANA. 'an die kreisauer hunde, 'nachtrag an die kreisauer hunde' and 'die verschiebung des mundes' from *kochanie ich habe brot gekauft* (kookbooks, 2005), 'dust bunnies' from *falsche freunde* (kookbooks, 2009), 'mappa' and 'kleine sternmullrede' from *meine schönste lengevitch* (kookbooks, 2013), all used with permission of the publisher. 'to the dogs of kreisau' and 'postscript to the kreisau dogs' translated by Brian Currid, first appeared on lyrikline.org; 'displacement of the mouth' translated by Grace Nissan, first appeared in *kochanie, today i bought bread* (World Poetry Books, 2023); 'stationary', 'dust bunnies vs wool mice' and 'little star-nosed mole speech' translated by Sophie Seita, first published in *Subsisters: Selected Poems* (Belladonna 2017), all reprinted with permission of the translators.

For all other poems and previously unpublished translations, copyright remains with the authors unless otherwise stated. Every effort has been made to trace copyright holders and we would be grateful to be notified of any errors or omissions.

Index of Poets

Yevgeniy Breyger	50, 51, 52, 115-6, 157, 164-5
Sonja vom Brocke	122, 133
Alexandru Bulucz	54, 92, 106, 107
Carolin Callies	35, 68
Ann Cotten	20-21, 26, 37, 94-96, 108, 182-3
Ulrike Draesner	154, 178-181, 185-6
Oswald Egger	89-90
Elke Erb	33, 47, 172, 184, 191
Daniel Falb	19, 36, 38, 104, 121, 129
Christian Filips	158, 173
Dinçer Güçyeter	58, 105, 155, 162-3
Martina Hefter	84, 85
Jayne-Ann Igel	55, 87, 114
Hendrik Jackson	57, 91, 110
Thomas Kling	22, 23, 73, 137, 138
Dagmara Kraus	128, 187-9
Birgit Kreipe	53, 88, 134-5, 139-140, 166
Nadja Küchenmeister	24, 99, 156
Jan Kuhlbrodt	71-72, 175-7
Georg Leß	25, 124, 174
Friederike Mayröcker	74, 83, 97
Christoph Meckel	70, 111, 123
Steffen Popp	18, 27, 49, 56, 86, 109, 112-3, 136
Kerstin Preiwuß	43
Monika Rinck	17, 32, 39, 69, 75, 78, 98, 167
Ulrike Almut Sandig	119-120
Sabine Scho	34, 79, 125-6, 130
Tom Schulz	28, 116, 152-3
Daniela Seel	59-61
Verena Stauffer	77
Ulf Stolterfoht	141-148
Sebastian Unger	67, 76, 127, 161
Anja Utler	40-42
Peter Waterhouse	44, 48, 66, 103, 159-160
Uljana Wolf	31, 65, 151, 171, 189, 190

Index of Translators

Shane Anderson	33, 47, 53, 59-61, 173, 19§
Kurt Beals	40-42
Paul-Henri Campbell	35, 68
Aimee Chor	24, 99, 156
Ann Cotten	20-21, 26, 37, 67, 76, 79-80, 94-6, 108, 182-3
Brian Currid	121, 189, 190
Andrew Duncan	22, 23, 73, 137-8
Joshua Daniel Edwin	128, 187-8
Christopher Fenwick	126
Gerald Fiebig	28, 116, 152-3
Iain Galbraith	44, 48, 66, 89-90, 103, 154, 159-160, 178-180, 185-6
Robert Gillett	19, 36, 38, 104
Nicholas Grindell	17, 32, 39, 69, 75, 78, 98, 167
Catherine Hales	34, 91, 122, 133-5, 139-141, 141-8, 166
Christian Hawkey	112-3, 131
Jayashree Hari Joshi	158
Alexander Kappe	25, 50-52, 57, 71-2, 110, 115, 127, 157, 161, 164-5, 174, 175-7
Karen Leeder	55, 84-5, 87, 112, 119-120, 130
Grace Nissan	31
Caroline Wilcox Reul	58, 105, 155, 162-3
Bradley Schmidt	18, 43, 49, 56, 70, 77, 86, 109, 111, 123, 125-6, 136
Jake Schneider	54, 92-3, 106-7
Joel Scott	88
Sophie Seita	65, 151, 171
Donna Stonecipher	22, 97
Lotta Thießen	88
Nicola Thomas	74, 83
Amy Visram	172, 184
Jana Maria Weiß	172, 184

www.ingramcontent.com/pod-product-compliance
Ingram Content Group UK Ltd.
Pitfield, Milton Keynes, MK11 3LW, UK
UKHW040714160925
7921UKWH00014B/212